# THE BUCKET SQUAD

## Teaching Children Kindness, Appreciation and Positive Behavior Through Bucket Filling

**Foreword by Carol McCloud,**
Author of
*Have You Filled A Bucket Today?*

**By Lisa K. Hansen, M.S.**

youth light inc.

© 2015 YouthLight, Inc.
Chapin, SC 29036

Design by Melody Taylor
Project Editing by Susan Bowman

ISBN: 978-1-59850-165-0

Library of Congress Number: 2014948703

10 9 8 7 6 5 4 3 2 1
Printed in the United States

# TABLE OF CONTENTS

**FOREWARD**

by Carol McCloud

Author of *Have You Filled a Bucket Today?* and *Bucket Fillers, Inc.*

I discovered bucketfilling in the 1990s when I attended an early childhood conference and was soon using the concept with great success in my work with preschool children. Never before had I seen children accept and understand a concept so quickly. They loved having their buckets filled with high fives and compliments. They especially loved to hear me tell them what terrific bucket fillers they were!

Fifteen years later, while discussing the merits of bucketfilling with another teacher, I wondered why no one had yet written a book to help children understand this concept. That night I wrote the first draft of the children's book, *Have You Filled a Bucket Today?* At the time I could not have dreamed how far and fast this life-enhancing concept would travel in just eight short years.

> **Each lesson of The Bucket Squad is clear-ly written, easy-to-follow, and includes:**
> > Objectives
> > Supplies Needed
> > Preparation
> > Opening Activity
> > Learning Activities
> > Closing Activity
> > Classroom Tip and a
> > Letter to Parent or Guardian (Bucket Squad News)

It wasn't long before I was wondering why no one had written a classroom or small group curriculum devoted to bucketfilling. The concept had been proven successful and powerful in elementary classrooms around the world. Teachers wanted something to help them teach the bucketfilling concept.

Enter Lisa Hansen with her guide, *The Bucket Squad*, which filled my bucket when I read it. I couldn't have been more enthusiastic about her book.

*The Bucket Squad* is a perfect guide for teaching children what it means to be a bucket filler. The lessons begin with the basics and advance to higher skills. There are tips for success and forms to record progress.

Lessons 1-3 explain what it means to fill buckets, your own as well as those of others. Lessons 4-6 teach the bucketfilling skills of listening, complimenting, cooperation and teamwork. Lessons 7-9 focus on the social/emotional skills of identifying feelings, awareness of others, overcoming negative thoughts, and solving problems in relationships. Lesson 10 is the Grand Finale: The celebration of everyone's bucketfilling accomplishments.

I am confident that your enthusiasm combined with the material in Lisa Hansen's wonderful book will help you guide your children as they discover the happy rewards of bucketfilling.

# INTRODUCTION

Carol McCloud's book, *Have You Filled a Bucket Today?*, is an effective social skills tool to use with children. The book introduces children to the concepts of *bucketfilling* and *bucketdipping*. Kids as young as four understand these ideas and are able to apply them in their interactions with peers.

As an elementary school counselor, I implemented Carol McCloud's books and ideas in my school. We adopted the language on a school-wide level and I reinforced the concepts in my classroom presentations. In fact, I believed in the usefulness of the message to such a degree, I decided to take her concepts and apply it to small group learning with students in my school. The bucketfilling language provided a wonderful foundation for social skills group work with my students. It was so successful I wanted to share it with other professionals, and as a result, I wrote the Bucket Squad Curriculum.

> **Bucketfilling skills include being friendly, listening, having good conversations, making and maintaining friendships, complimenting others, standing up for your own needs in a respectful way and developing self-confidence.**

Elementary counselors, social workers, classroom teachers, special education teachers and school psychologists spend a lot of their time proactively helping young students develop interpersonal skills that are necessary to be successful in school and life. These skills include being friendly, listening, having good conversations, making and maintaining friendships, complimenting others, standing up for your own needs in a respectful way, and developing self-confidence. All are examples of bucketfilling skills.

*The Bucket Squad* curriculum will give other professionals working with students the ability to introduce, practice, and reinforce these skills in a way that is both enjoyable and highly effective. The curriculum guide is written to be delivered in a small group format, but it can be easily adjusted for teachers who want to use these lessons with their entire class. Tips on how to adjust the lessons are included throughout the guide. The curriculum also provides weekly letters for parent communication. Parents are able to reinforce the language and skills easily within their home environment.

The curriculum has been successfully followed in schools prior to this publishing and I am confident that your students will benefit from its introduction as well. The following pages will provide all the information you need to create and implement a successful *Bucket Squad* in your school.

Good Luck!

# BUCKET SQUAD OBJECTIVES

The *Bucket Squad* curriculum uses an educational small group model that can also be easily adapted as large group classroom lessons to create a positive bucketfilling classroom environment. The curriculum is appropriate for elementary-aged children. The following is a list of objectives for the program:

- Recognize and encourage the individuality of participants.
- Identify the talents, personal qualities, pro-social skills and challenges of the participants.
- Educate participants about various bucketfilling behaviors.
- Practice the learned bucketfilling skills.
- Encourage through reinforcement group members who use bucketfilling techniques and behaviors.
- Increase empathy.
- Increase self-confidence in children.
- Teach children how to protect their self-esteem.
- Positively impact the school climate as a whole.

## Classroom Tips

Teachers or other classroom leaders can follow the weekly curriculum and create an entire class of bucket fillers! Tips will be included throughout this guide on how to adjust the activities for use in the classroom. Look for the bucket symbol above at the end of each weekly lesson outline.

## Tips for Successful Groups with Children
### Who should participate?
Participation in this group benefits all children. Enhancing and reinforcing pro-social skills is important for everyone and all students can grow from the experience. This group can be especially helpful for students who are struggling with self-confidence *OR* for students who need extra help making and maintaining friendships. The curriculum can also be useful for a teacher to establish a positive peer environment in the classroom.

### Small Group Size and Composition
Although this curriculum can work with various age groups, it is best to form small groups of children who are close to the same age. For example, Kindergarten students and 1st graders could meet together, but it would be difficult to make a group work well with Kindergarten and 3rd graders together because of the wide variance of intellectual and emotional development. However, older students can serve as peer helpers if the facilitator needs to consolidate older and younger grades into one group.

Ideally, groups should consist of 6 to 8 children per group. It is helpful to mix the needs of the group members. Mixing a few children who have low self-confidence, but good social skills with those who are struggling socially can create a successful group composition. This allows the students to increase their self-confidence by being positive peer models for their group mates who are working on specific bucketfilling skills.

## Small Group Session Framework

The group should meet weekly for ten weeks. Everything you will need to start is included in this curriculum. The lessons consist of weekly goals, a list of necessary materials, a description of activities with their estimated time periods, weekly bucketfilling assignments and a weekly letter to parents/teachers.

## Parent/Teacher Involvement

Children experience positive changes in their interpersonal relationships when both parents and teachers are involved. The skills learned in the small group should be transferred and reinforced outside of the group setting in order for long-lasting change to take place and for self-esteem to grow. *The Bucket Squad* curriculum accomplishes this through a weekly Bucket Chart where students track their progress and are held accountable to that progress. A letter to parents is also included for each session so parents can reinforce the bucketfilling behaviors at home.

## Pre-/Post-Assessment

In order to chart the effectiveness of the program, a pre-/post-assessment for each student is included in this workbook. There is also a pre-/post-assessment that parents and teachers can complete. Give the pre-assessment either prior to or during week one and the post-assessment during week ten. If it's more convenient or helpful, you can also create an assessment at the beginning and end of each weekly session to demonstrate the learning that took place each week.

# BUCKET SQUAD INVITATION

Dear Parent(s)/Guardian(s) of_____,

Your child has the opportunity to participate in a small group at our school. All group members will learn about the concept of filling buckets by reading the book, *Have You Filled a Bucket Today?*, by Carol McCloud. (A description of bucketfilling is included on the back side of this letter.)

During each small group meeting we will work on one way to fill our classmates', friends' and teachers' buckets. Then The Squad will be asked to use that specific skill to become a bucket filler. The ways Squad members will fill buckets include using friendly greetings, listening to others, giving genuine compliments, being a team player by taking turns and cooperating, and by using peaceful problem solving skills. Students participating in this group will have a special role in this school. They will not only become skilled bucket fillers, but as a team, they will also be actively contributing to a positive school climate. Each time they work to fill buckets, their own buckets will also be filled, promoting a strong sense of self-esteem and positive peer relationships for the Squad members.

The small group will meet weekly. Following each group session, I will send a letter home so you are aware of the bucketfilling skill and assignment of the week. You may even notice the students working to fill buckets at home!

If you would like your child to participate in the Bucket Squad, please complete the permission slip below along with the adult pre-assessment form and have your child return it by the date listed. If you have any questions or concerns, please feel free to contact me.

Sincerely,

_____

✂ - - - - - - - - - - - - - - - - - - - - - - - - - - - - - - - - - - - - - - - - - - - - - - - - - - - - - - -

My child, _____, has permission to participate in the

Bucket Squad. (Please return by _____.)

# WHAT IS BUCKETFILLING?

"Bucketfilling" is based on the book, *Have You Filled A Bucket Today?*, written by Carol McCloud. The story explains that everyone is born with an invisible bucket. The bucket has one purpose only, to hold your good thoughts and good feelings about yourself. The book explains that you feel very happy and good when your bucket is full, and you feel very sad and lonely when your bucket is empty. In order to have a full bucket, you need other people to fill your bucket and other people need you to fill theirs. Students learn that they can fill other peoples' buckets when they say or do something kind, smile at classmates, are helpful, and try their best. Participants also learn that sometimes people can be "bucket dippers." This is when someone dips into a bucket and takes out someone's good feelings, for example, by making fun of someone, saying or doing mean things or ignoring a classmate. I encourage you to reinforce this concept in your home by using the bucketfilling/bucketdipping language.

The bucket has one purpose only, to hold your good thoughts and good feelings about yourself.

# THE BUCKET SQUAD
## Student Pre-/Post-Assessment

**1.** What is bucketfilling?

_____

_____

**2.** Name two ways to be a bucketfiller:

a._____

b. _____

**3.** Name four parts of our body that we use when we are being a good listener.

a._____

b. _____

c._____

d. _____

**4.** What is bucketdipping?

_____

_____

**5.** Give an example of an "It Dips" message using all 3 parts.

a._____

b. _____

c._____

**6.** On a scale from 1 to 3, how do you feel about being a part of the Bucket Squad?

**1**  🙁    **2**  😔    **3**  🙂

**7.** Show how full your bucket is today using the bucket drawing. (Older kids can indicate the level of their bucket contents by drawing a line on or coloring their bucket and younger kids can put a smile, straight line, or sad face onto the bucket to show how their bucket currently looks/feels to them).

# HOW FULL IS YOUR BUCKET TODAY?

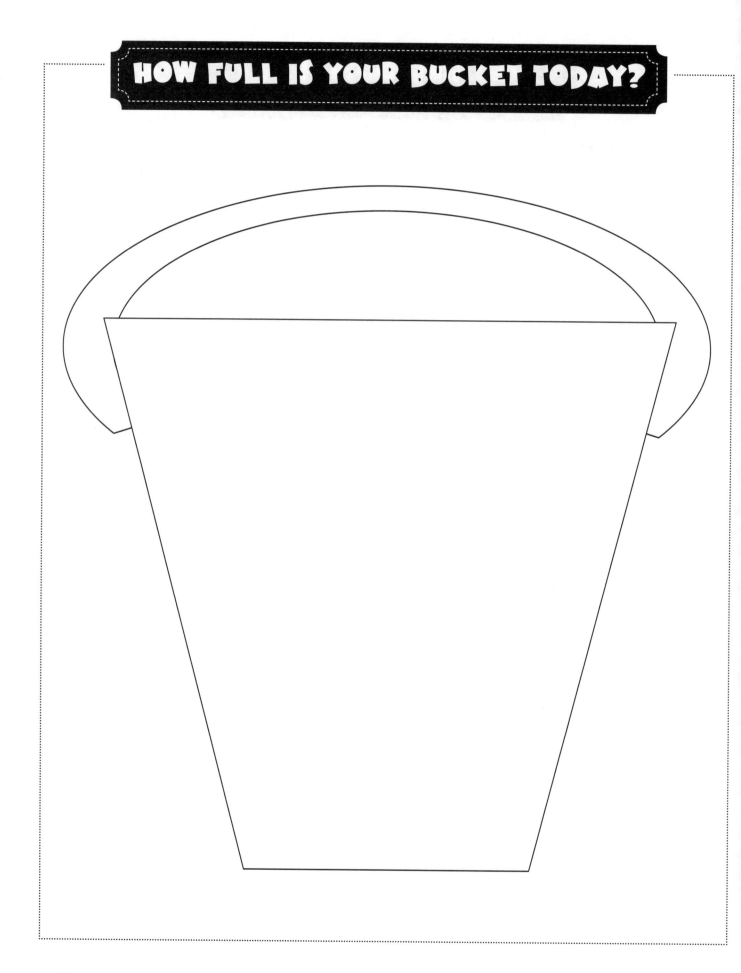

# ADULT PRE-ASSESSMENT

Your name: _____

Child/student's name: _____

Please circle the number below that best describes your child/student.

**1.** S/he is able to recognize positives in others and give compliments.

| Hardly ever | Sometimes | Often |
|:---:|:---:|:---:|
| 1 | 2 | 3 |

**2.** S/he listens well to others.

| Hardly ever | Sometimes | Often |
|:---:|:---:|:---:|
| 1 | 2 | 3 |

**3.** S/he cooperates with peers by taking turns and working together.

| Hardly ever | Sometimes | Often |
|:---:|:---:|:---:|
| 1 | 2 | 3 |

**4.** S/he makes and keeps friends.

| Hardly ever | Sometimes | Often |
|:---:|:---:|:---:|
| 1 | 2 | 3 |

**5.** S/he is able to solve conflicts well.

| Hardly ever | Sometimes | Often |
|:---:|:---:|:---:|
| 1 | 2 | 3 |

**6.** S/he uses the bucket language to describe how s/he is feeling or how others are treating her/him.

| Hardly ever | Sometimes | Often |
|:---:|:---:|:---:|
| 1 | 2 | 3 |

I think my child's/student's bucket is (circle your answer)

**Nearly empty**          **Somewhat full**          **Full**

Comments/Feedback: _____

_____

_____

# ADULT POST-ASSESSMENT

Your name: _____

Child/student's name: _____

Please circle the number below that best describes your child/student.

**1.** S/he is able to recognize positives in others and give compliments.

| Hardly ever | Sometimes | Often |
|:---:|:---:|:---:|
| 1 | 2 | 3 |

**2.** S/he listens well to others.

| Hardly ever | Sometimes | Often |
|:---:|:---:|:---:|
| 1 | 2 | 3 |

**3.** S/he cooperates with peers by taking turns and working together.

| Hardly ever | Sometimes | Often |
|:---:|:---:|:---:|
| 1 | 2 | 3 |

**4.** S/he makes and keeps friends.

| Hardly ever | Sometimes | Often |
|:---:|:---:|:---:|
| 1 | 2 | 3 |

**5.** S/he is able to solve conflicts well.

| Hardly ever | Sometimes | Often |
|:---:|:---:|:---:|
| 1 | 2 | 3 |

**6.** S/he uses the bucket language to describe how s/he is feeling or how others are treating her/him.

| Hardly ever | Sometimes | Often |
|:---:|:---:|:---:|
| 1 | 2 | 3 |

I think my child's/student's bucket is (circle your answer)

**Nearly empty**          **Somewhat full**          **Full**

Comments/Feedback: _____

_____

_____

# THE BUCKET SQUAD KICK OFF
## Skill Learned
### What it means to fill buckets.

## OBJECTIVES:

Participants will:

⟐ Get to know each other's names

⟐ Create group rules and guidelines

⟐ Learn about the bucketfilling concept

⟐ Decorate their very own bucket

## SUPPLIES NEEDED:

⟐ A small ball

⟐ The book, *Have You Filled a Bucket Today?*, by Carol McCloud (available through YouthLight, Inc.)

⟐ Poster paper

⟐ Markers, pencils or pens

⟐ A bucket for each student (can be commonly found at a dollar store or other discount retailer OR use large plastic cups and pipe cleaners to make buckets)

⟐ Decorating supplies (markers, paint pens, stickers)

⟐ Letter for parents/teacher (Bucket Squad News)

⟐ Camera

## PREPARATION:

Before the group meeting, gather supplies and read through the curriculum. This is the first group session and it is important to be prepared. The session will establish expectations, build enthusiasm, and develop rapport among group members. It is helpful to:

⟐ Have bucket-making supplies visible.

⟐ Make copies of the Bucket Squad News ahead of time. (page 21)

## OPENING ACTIVITY: (5 – 10 minutes)

After welcoming everyone to the Bucket Squad's first meeting, play a name game to help ensure all participants learn each other's names. Depending on the age of the children in your group, you have a choice of two versions of this game to play. Younger children may need your help coming up with words to go along with their names.

## K-2nd Grades

» Sit in a circle

» Explain to everyone that you are going to practice each others' names by saying a word that starts with the same letter sound as your name. For example, if your name is Jack, you might say, "Hi, my name is Jumping Jack!"

» You begin, say your name, and then give a ball to the person on the left. The next student says your description and name, his description and name, and then hands the ball off to the next student in the circle. For example, "This is Jumping Jack, and my name is Smiley Sarah." That student repeats your description and name, the previous participant's description and name, and then her description and name. You continue this pattern around the circle until the ball comes back to you. At that time, you repeat all the descriptions and names in the circle.

## 3rd-5th Grades

» First, play the game above either with descriptions or without.

» Then, have students stand up and scramble the circle.

» Replay the original name game with a new order or play using the option below.

» This time, roll the ball to a student across from you in the circle. She should say your name and then her name. She should then roll the ball towards another student, saying that student's name. Continue this until everyone has had a turn and been named.

## GROUP GUIDELINES: (5 minutes)

Explain to the students that the group needs guidelines on how they treat one another while they are together. It can help to say to the students, "I want to make sure you look forward to coming to the Bucket Squad each week. How should we treat each other for this to be a fun, comfortable and helpful time together?" Allow the kids to come up with their own ideas and help them to paraphrase the rules. For example, if a student said "no hitting," you might write "keep your hands to yourself." Write the rules on poster paper and have the students sign their names signifying their commitment to the group guidelines. Here is a suggested list to guide you through the process:

» Be kind, no put-downs

» Keep your hands to yourself/respect each other's space

» Take turns talking and listening

» Participate in activities

» Right to Pass—each student has the right to "pass" if s/he is uncomfortable answering a question.

# LEARNING ACTIVITIES: WHAT IS BUCKETFILLING? (20 minutes)

**PART 1: Read one of the following books by Carol McCloud:**

K-1st:  *Fill a Bucket*

2nd-5th: *Have You Filled a Bucket Today?*

**PART 2: Decorate and Discuss!**

Explain to the Bucket Squad that they are going to have the chance to make their own bucket. Their buckets are an important tool and the Squad will use them each week. (The group leader should keep the buckets after this session to use during future weekly sessions.)

⟩ Have students sit at a table

⟩ Cover the table if using paint pens or permanent markers

⟩ Give a bucket to each group member

**Notes:**

1. Plastic buckets can often be found at dollar stores or discount stores.

2. Buckets can be made from large plastic cups/containers and pipe cleaners.

   a. Use a push pin to poke two holes on opposite sides of the cup/container.

   b. Thread the pipe cleaner through the holes and twist to form a handle.

   c. Lay out supplies like markers, paint pens, and stickers to decorate the buckets.

Discuss the story while the students are decorating their buckets:

- How does a person feel when his or her bucket is full?
- How does a person feel when his or her bucket is empty?
- How does someone get a full bucket?
- What kinds of actions can people take to fill each other's buckets?
- How important do you think it is to be a bucket filler?
- If you worked extra hard to fill people's buckets, what would happen to your bucket?
- How would our school look or feel if everyone filled buckets?
- How would you like to fill people's buckets each week?

**Important:** Help the students understand that they have been selected to be a part of a Bucket Squad in your school. They have a very important job to do. You are the coach and they are your team! Together, you will help the school be a better place, one bucket at a time. And because of all the kindness they will spread, the team members' buckets will also be fuller.

**PART 3:** With a digital camera, take a photograph of each of the group members holding their bucket.

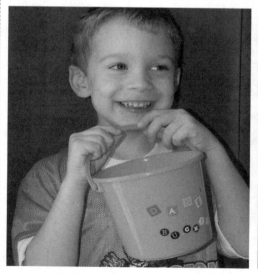 

# CLOSING ACTIVITY: (3 minutes)

**K-1st Grade Option: The Bucket Squad Cheer!**

**Directions:** (Stand in a circle and follow the order below)

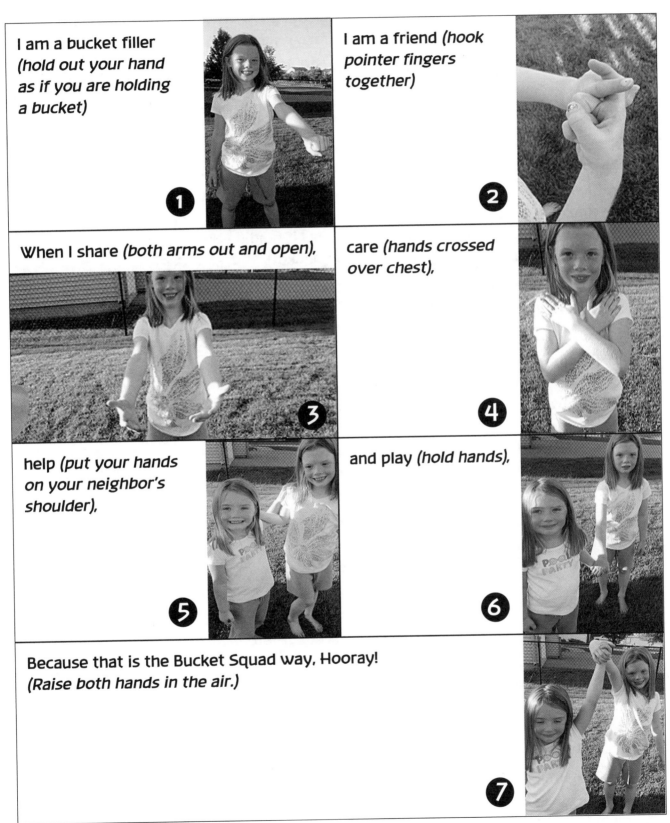

I am a bucket filler *(hold out your hand as if you are holding a bucket)*

**1**

I am a friend *(hook pointer fingers together)*

**2**

When I share *(both arms out and open),*

**3**

care *(hands crossed over chest),*

**4**

help *(put your hands on your neighbor's shoulder),*

**5**

and play *(hold hands),*

**6**

Because that is the Bucket Squad way, Hooray! *(Raise both hands in the air.)*

**7**

## 2nd-5th Grade Option:
### The Bucket Squad Handshake!

**Directions:** Pair up the kids and either do the following handshake or allow them to create their own Squad handshake.

| | |
|---|---|
| Face your partner.  | Each partner holds up the right hand and slaps the other's palm. 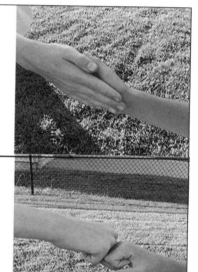 |
| Then turn your hands and slap your right hands on their back side.  | Form your right hand into a fist (as if holding a bucket), and bump knuckles with your partner. |

## Parent/Teacher Communication:

Send home the parent letter with each child. You can also make an extra copy for the children's teachers so they are aware of the group's weekly activities and goals.

 ## CLASSROOM TIPS:

If you are using this curriculum to teach and reinforce bucketfilling in the classroom, here are a few tips to personalize this lesson:

Read the book, *Have You Filled a Bucket Today?*, to your entire class and discuss bucketfilling. Tell your class that you want them to become a class full of bucket fillers! Let your students know that they will be doing special activities each week to learn and practice bucketfilling.

Create a classroom bucket. Select a large bucket or jar and decorate it. The class bucket will be used in conjunction with a bucketfilling chart during later weeks. The classroom bucket will monitor and reinforce bucketfilling behaviors in your classroom.

You could also have students create their own individual buckets if you wish. The buckets can simply be used as decoration in the class. You can hang them from the ceiling of the classroom or make a wall display. Some teachers have also utilized these buckets in an interactive way by having students fill each other's buckets throughout the weeks with positive messages. However, the classroom curriculum will not be focusing on the use of individual buckets.

Use the bucketfilling cheer or handshake described in this lesson to create unity and a sense of belonging in your classroom. Finally, adapt the Bucket Squad News to complement your classroom lesson. Send the letter home or post an update on your classroom website!

# BUCKET SQUAD NEWS
## SESSION ONE

**Dear Parent or Guardian:**

Today was the first group meeting with the bucket squad. We participated in a lot of fun activities to get our team off to a great start! First, we played a game that helped us to learn each others' names. Then, we created group rules to ensure our time together is safe and enjoyable for everyone. After that, we read a great story called, *Have You Filled a Bucket Today?*, by Carol McCloud.

Once everyone understood the concepts behind bucketfilling, we learned about our special job as a team of bucket fillers in our school. This is important because it will help our school become a respectful and safe place. Being a bucket filler will also make us feel great!

The special project today was decorating our very own bucket. We will be watching our buckets fill up each week. This will provide a concrete way of reinforcing how filling other people's buckets also fills our own.

Our newsletter, "Bucket Squad News," will be sent home each week to update you on the Bucket Squad's weekly meeting and goals. Please use the contact information listed below if you have any comments, questions, or concerns.


Sincerely,


Your Name, Title_____

Phone: _____

Email: _____

**At Home Discussion:** Ask your child to explain bucketfilling to you. What is her/his favorite part of the first group meeting?

# WE ARE THE BUCKET SQUAD
## Skill Learned
### Liking me keeps my bucket full.

## OBJECTIVES:

⧽ Participants will:

⧽ Review the squad members' names and group rules

⧽ Review bucketfilling

⧽ Identify Squad members' unique qualities and talents

## SUPPLIES NEEDED:

⧽ Group rules from Session One

⧽ Squad members' buckets from Session One

⧽ 3 plastic cups (or other container of your choice)

⧽ Craft sticks for each group member

⧽ Photograph of each group member from last week

⧽ Glue stick and scissors

⧽ Copies of "List of Qualities and Talents" (one per squad member)

⧽ Letter for parents/teacher (Bucket Squad News)

## PREPARATION:

Before the group meeting, gather supplies and read through the curriculum. It is helpful to make several preparations prior to the group meeting. Here are a few suggestions:

**1.** Copy the "List of Qualities and Talents" for each group member. You can save time during group by cutting them into strips ahead of time (colored paper looks nice).

**2.** Copy the Bucket Squad News for each student to take home.

**3.** Assemble check-in buckets. See directions below:

⧽ Gather clear plastic cups.

⧽ Use markers or cut out the pictures below.

⧽ Create one bucket that is full and happy, one that is ½ full, and one that is nearly empty and sad.

# GROUP CHECK IN: HOW FULL IS MY BUCKET? (15 minutes)

**PART 1:** Give each group member a craft stick and a copy of their individual photo from the last session. Have the kids cut out images of their heads or their whole body outline from the photograph. Glue the photograph to the craft stick. Ask the kids to write their names on the sticks with markers. While the kids are working on their sticks, have a discussion about buckets.

⟫ What did we learn about buckets last week?
- Everyone has a bucket.
- A bucket holds our good thoughts and good feelings.
- We can fill other people's buckets by being kind, helpful, and friendly.
- Sometimes people dip into other people's buckets.

⟫ If someone has a full bucket, what does that mean?
- A person with a full bucket has a lot of good thoughts and feelings.
- They are happy.

⟫ If someone has a bucket that isn't very full, what does that mean?
- People with an empty bucket may not feel very good about themselves and might be feeling left out or disliked.
- Sometimes kids with empty buckets dip into others' buckets to try to take their good thoughts and good feelings, but that doesn't make them happy.
- People with empty buckets need other people to fill their buckets.

**PART 2:** Teach the students that they will have an opportunity each week to show how full their own bucket is. This is a way to check-in with the group. Place the three buckets you prepared earlier in the middle of the table. Have the students use their sticks to show how their buckets look. They should pick the bucket that most resembles how they feel and place their stick in that cup. For example, do they have a lot of good thoughts and feelings? Are they feeling just so-so? Or do they have few positive feelings today? This can be a check-in each week that gives you a snapshot of how your group members are feeling about themselves. It also teaches and reinforces the idea that their buckets may look different from each other, and change on different days, depending on what has happened throughout the day. For example, the way others treat us, and the way we treat ourselves affects our buckets.

**K-1st Grades:** Have the students sit in a circle. You can lead them through the check-in process by singing this song. It creates routine and helps the younger children to wait for their turn and listen intently to one another.

## HOW ARE YOU? (This is a repeat-after-me song sung to the tune of *Three Blind Mice*)

How are you? **(Leader)**

How are you? **(Kids)**

So, how are you? **(Leader)**

So, how are you? **(Kids)**

I hope your bucket is full today. **(Leader)**

I hope your bucket is full today. **(Kids)**

I just can't wait to hear what you say. **(Leader)**

I just can't wait to hear what you say. **(Kids)**

Is it low, so-so or full today? **(Leader)**

Is it low, so-so or full today? **(Kids)**

So, how are you? **(Leader)**

So, how are you? **(Kids)**

Leader asks, "How are you, (insert name of group member)?"

*Keep repeating the song until everyone has had the opportunity to check-in with their sticks.*

**2nd-5th Grades:** An alternative for older kids to check in is to have the group members take turns using cotton pom-poms, paper strips, marbles, feathers, foam shapes, or any other creative object to fill a check-in bucket until it reflects the way s/he feels. (The higher the bucket is filled, the better s/he feels.)

> **Important:** Reinforce with the kids that by being a part of the Bucket Squad, they are going to have the chance to not only fill other people's buckets, but they are also going to see and feel their own buckets fill up. They will learn how the way they treat other people and the way other people treat them affects the way they feel. This will help to build the important interpersonal skill of empathy.

## OPENING ACTIVITY: (5 to 7 minutes)

### Welcome everyone back to the Bucket Squad!

Take out the rules that were compiled in Session One and review them with the group. Hang them up so they are in clear sight.

Play "**I like to…**"
Directions for play:

- Stand in a circle.

- Ask the students to go around the circle and answer this question by showing an action without words.

- The first person might say, "My name is Jim and I like to…" and then make the motion of swimming without words. Then, the next person would say, "That is Jim and he likes to… (repeating the motion of swimming without words), and my name is Jennifer and I like to… (making the motion of climbing). Then, the next squad member says, "Jim likes to... (repeating swimming motion), Jennifer likes to... (with climbing motion), and I like to…"

- This game continues until it returns to the leader

- The leader should end the game by repeating everyone's actions and then add, "I like to… (with the motion of filling buckets).

## LEARNING ACTIVITIES: What do I like about me? (15 minutes)

Using the list of Qualities and Talents found on the following page, help students identify qualities they believe make them special and that they are proud of having. The leader should make a copy ahead of time for each group member.

**K-2nd Grades:** Tell the students you are going to read a list of qualities and talents out loud. While you read it, ask them to think about whether the words describe them. Reinforce that it is almost impossible for someone to have all of these traits and talents. Ask the students to pick at least 5 of them. Then, read the qualities/talents one at a time. Have the students raise their hand if the words describe them. Then give the students that slip of paper. (It is helpful to cut the paper strips ahead of time.)

**3rd-5th Grades:** You can conduct the process in the same way as described above or you can ask the students to read through their personal lists of qualities. They should choose 5 to 10 words that they think describe them. Older students can cut out their words. There are also two blanks so the kids can add attributes that are not listed. Share the qualities they chose with the rest of the group and ask the students to explain why they picked each.

**All Grades:** Have each group member roll up his or her pieces of paper listing the chosen attributes and talents. Then place the rolled-up papers into their week one buckets!

> **Important:** Remind the Bucket Squad that a bucket holds all your good thoughts and good feelings about yourself. Although other people can fill your bucket by being kind and friendly to you, a bucket only stays full when you like who you are. One way to do this is to remember the qualities and talents that make you special.

## Qualities and Talents:

Ask the kids, "Who remembers everyone's names from last time? Great! Today, we're going to play another fun game to help us remember everyone's name and learn a little more about each other."

| | |
|---|---|
| Friendly | Smart/Intelligent |
| Caring | Athletic |
| Helpful | Musical |
| Shares easily | Good listener |
| Sensitive | Responsible |
| Organized | Artistic |
| Creative | Trustworthy |
| Adventurous/Likes to try new things | Funny/Good sense of humor |
| Loyal | Perseverance/Doesn't give up easily |

## CLOSING ACTIVITY: (3 minutes)

**K-1st Grade Option:** *The Bucket Squad Cheer!*

**2nd-5th Grade Option:** *The Bucket Squad Handshake!*

{ **Ask kids to pair up with a different partner this week to do the handshake!**
**Send home the Bucket Squad News.** }

## CLASSROOM TIPS:

If you are following this curriculum to teach and reinforce bucketfilling in the classroom, here are a few tips to adjust this lesson:

Even if your students already know each other well, playing the game of "I like to" can help them learn more about one another and find attributes they may have in common with others. It is a great classroom game!

One part you may want to change is the check-in activity. Your students might feel vulnerable if asked to show how full their buckets are in front of their classmates. However, you may find it beneficial to know this information as a teacher. You can easily adapt this activity by handing out a paper copy of a bucket (see Appendix A) and asking the students to color in the bucket to show how full their bucket is while they are at school. (If you are concerned about behavior or social interaction and its impact at lunch, recess, or other group functions of the school day, you can ask specific kids to show you how their bucket feels during those times.) This is a great way for you to be aware of which kids might need your individual help and who might benefit from additional care.

Next, use the qualities and talents activity in the classroom. Lead a class discussion on people's list of Qualities and Talents. Either use the handout or brainstorm to create a list as a class. Discuss how talents and qualities affect people's feelings. It is important for students to realize that the way they think about themselves also impacts how they feel. Many wonderful children's books can additionally be included to reinforce the concept of self-esteem and enrich the learning and classroom environment. One of my favorites for younger students is *Stand Tall, Molly Lou Melon* by Patty Lovell. You will notice that the bucket philosophy can easily be applied to many of the stories you will read in class. During class discussions, ask the students about the characters' buckets in the story. Who is being a bucket filler? Who is being a bucket dipper? Finally, edit the Bucket Squad News to reflect your classroom activities for the week. Send it out to parents or post it on your classroom website.

**Dear Parent or Guardian:**

The Bucket Squad had a great time today. We started our meeting by playing a game called, "I like to…" We took turns sharing what we like to do by acting it out without words. For example, someone in the group who likes to swim made a swimming motion with his or her arms. This also helped us learn more about each other's interests.

Then, we cut out a picture of ourselves that we took last week. We glued it onto a stick and placed the stick in one of three buckets: a bucket that is almost empty and looks sad, a bucket that is half full and looks as if it is feeling so-so, and a bucket that appears full and happy. We each chose the bucket that most accurately reflected the way our own buckets look. We will do this each week.

After that, we spent time talking about the personal qualities and talents that make each of the group members special. Each child had the opportunity to choose qualities they have and discuss the qualities that they like about themselves. Then, they used the slips of paper these attributes were written on to begin filling the buckets they made during the first week.

Students were reminded that a bucket holds all your good thoughts and good feelings about yourself. Although other people can fill your bucket by being kind and friendly to you, we also feel good when we remember the talents and qualities we have that make each of us special.

We ended our group with the Bucket Squad cheer or handshake!

Sincerely,

Your Name, Title_____

Phone: _____

Email: _____

 **At Home Discussion:** Into which bucket did you place your stick? What are some of the abilities and traits you said you liked about yourself or are good at? Show me the Bucket Squad Cheer or Handshake.

# THE FRIENDLY BUCKET SQUAD
## Skill Learned
### Being friendly fills buckets.

## OBJECTIVES:

Participants will:

⯁ Review their own unique qualities & talents

⯁ Brainstorm to create a list of ways they can be bucket fillers

⯁ Practice friendly greetings

## SUPPLIES NEEDED:

⯁ Group rules from Session One

⯁ Group buckets from Session One

⯁ Check-in buckets and check-in sticks from Session Two

⯁ Skittles® candy and question prompts

⯁ Small cups, plastic baggies, or cups for Skittles®

⯁ Poster paper

⯁ Markers

⯁ Bucket Chart

⯁ Puppets (optional)

⯁ Letter for parents/teacher (Bucket Squad News)

## PREPARATION:

Before the group meeting, gather supplies and read through the curriculum. You may find it helpful to make several preparations prior to the group meeting. Here are a few suggestions:

**1.** Have the check-in buckets and check-in sticks out upon the students' arrival.

**2.** Divide the Skittles® so that each group member has one of each color. Place them in your choice of small cups, plastic baggies, or on napkins.

**3.** Copy the bucket chart and The Bucket Squad News (one for each Squad member).

## GROUP CHECK-IN: HOW FULL IS MY BUCKET? (5 to 10 minutes)

Using the check-in buckets and craft sticks from session two, have group members check-in. Sing the "How Are You?" song with younger kids.

This week's check-in goals:

⯁ Show that our buckets can change.

⯁ Conducting a weekly check-in helps you know if any group members' buckets are consistently empty.

※ Offer a chance to brainstorm with the Squad to find ways to increase their good feelings.

※ Review the attributes the kids said they liked about themselves last week. How does remembering our special qualities and talents help to fill our buckets?

## OPENING ACTIVITY: (10 minutes)

**The Bucket Squad Skittles Game:** Use the Skittle Game to help the kids get to know one another better and become more comfortable within the group setting. Each group member gets one of each color of candy (Skittles®). Before they can eat their Skittles, they need to answer questions about themselves.

※ **RED:** What is your favorite food? Least favorite food?

※ **ORANGE:** What is your favorite game to play?
(You can specify board game, video game or sport.)

※ **GREEN:** Name one thing you like about yourself.
(One talent/attribute they added to their bucket last week.)

※ **PURPLE:** How many brothers and sisters do you have?

※ **YELLOW:** Which Skittle flavor is your favorite?

## LEARNING ACTIVITIES: (25 minutes)

**Say to the group:** "Last time, we talked about what we like about ourselves. We picked out some talents and qualities we each have that make us feel good. We then put those special qualities into our buckets. This helped us see that one of the ways we begin to fill our buckets is with our own positive thoughts and feelings about ourselves. Although this is a great start to having a full bucket, we can also add to our own buckets by helping other people fill their buckets. Today, we are going to begin brainstorming ways to fill other people's buckets. Then, each week we will work hard as a team to fill as many buckets as possible. What an amazing difference this team will make in our school!"

Brainstorm to create a list of bucketfilling actions with the students.

Using poster paper or a whiteboard, write down the responses of your group. This process will help children take ownership in the plans of the group. However, since the group sessions are pre-planned, it helps to lead them toward a list that looks similar to the following example.

### Ways We Can Be Bucket Fillers

※ Be friendly
※ Listen and pay attention to my teacher, parents, and friends
※ Give genuine compliments to others
※ Be a team player by taking turns and being a good sport
※ Solve problems without bucket dipping
※ Be a good friend to others and include other kids in my activities

**This week's bucketfilling action:** *Friendly Greetings*
Explain to the students that from now on, they will be working as a team to fill other people's buckets using the list they just created. This week, they are going to start with being friendly.

**K-2nd Grades:** For younger students it may be beneficial to lead them through the following discussion by acting out both friendly and unfriendly examples of each of the components of greetings listed below. Have the children give you a "thumbs up" if what you are doing is friendly and a "thumbs down" if it is not.

**3rd-5th Grades:** Lead the kids through a discussion on these responses and allow them to come up with some of the examples on their own.

Ask the kids:

❧ **What does being friendly look like?**
- Smiling
  – Have everyone smile.
- Looking the other person in the eyes
  – Turn to your neighbor, smile and make sure you are looking straight at them when you do.
- Maintaining and respecting personal space
  – Leader should show an example of appropriate space. For example, smiling and using eye contact is great, but if you were to do it two inches from another person's face, it would be uncomfortable.

❧ **What does a friendly greeting sound like?**
- Tone of voice
  – Leader should give examples of different tones of voice and have kids pick out which tones sound friendly.
- Confident volume
  – Leader should give examples of various volume levels and have kids choose which volume sounded the most pleasant.

❧ **What are some examples of a friendly greeting?**
- Saying, "Hello."
- Waving at someone.
- Giving a high five.
- Giving a handshake or appropriate hug.

❧ **What would be bucketdipping greetings?**
- Ignoring someone when they say hello.
- Invading their personal space or being very loud.
- Slapping hands too hard or pushing someone you see.
- Hugging someone that doesn't want to be hugged.

## Practice Friendly Greetings:

- Pair students up for practice.

- First, have them envision a way to greet one another that might dip into someone's bucket.
  - The pairs should practice acting out their unfriendly greeting.

- Second, have them envision a way to greet one another that is friendly, using eye contact, appropriate volume, space, and tone. The pairs should practice acting out their friendly greeting.

- Have the pairs role-play for the rest of the group. Allow each pair to take a turn showing both the bucketdipping greeting and the bucketfilling one!
  - Talk about the difference.

### Options:

- K-2nd: Use puppets to demonstrate the friendly greetings.

- 3rd-5th: You may want to go further with the role-plays and have the students practice handshakes and giving appropriate introductions.

## BUCKET CHART: (5 minutes)
### Weekly Goal: Fill buckets with friendly greetings!

Each week, the Bucket Squad will be receiving a bucket chart to take with them (see Appendix A). The team's goal for this week is to use friendly greetings to fill a lot of buckets! They can list an "X" or color in a square on their bucket chart for each friendly greeting they give. When a teacher or other adult catches them using bucketfilling greetings, they can also cross off a square on the child's bucket chart. The team should bring the chart with them to the next bucket squad meeting. They will probably fill up the chart quickly this week. This is a positive way to start the group and the kids will feel successful.

## CLOSING ACTIVITY: (3 minutes)
**K-1st Grade Option:** *The Bucket Squad Cheer!*

**2nd-5th Grade Option:** *The Bucket Squad Handshake!*

{ **Ask kids to pair up with a different partner this week to do the handshake!** }
**Send home the Bucket Squad News.**

## CLASSROOM TIPS:

If you are using this curriculum to teach and reinforce bucketfilling in the classroom, here are a few tips to adjust this lesson:

This lesson is easily adapted to the classroom without much modification. The role-plays and discussion can be done in the classroom as a written exercise. The only modification you may want to consider is how you will reinforce bucket-filling behaviors in your classroom. Here are some suggestions:

*Being friendly is a cornerstone upon which to build social skills, make friends, and help to create a compassionate environment.*

Use a large bucket chart on a classroom wall. Draw this on a piece of tag board or create one on an electronic white board.

Determine how you will record friendly greetings. Having students report to you each day can be quite time consuming. Your class can earn 1 to 5 squares depending on how often you notice friendly greetings throughout the day. If it is a large number, then the class gets five squares; and if they are dipping or not being friendly to one another throughout the day, they will earn less as a class.

This is an easy week but it is so important to reinforce the power of being friendly. It is a cornerstone upon which to build social skills, make friends, and help to create a compassionate environment. It is also something that we sometimes forget to reinforce because it is a basic expectation of our culture. But, by forgetting to reinforce and practice it, we also sometimes downplay the importance of friendliness. What a kind group you will have this week in your classroom! Edit the Bucket Squad News to reflect your classroom activities for the week. Send it out to parents or post it on your classroom website.

**Dear Parent or Guardian:**

We started our meeting by playing the Bucket Squad Skittles® Game. For each color of Skittles® candy, we said something about ourselves, like what our favorite food or color is. It was great to learn more about each other and discover qualities we might have in common. After that, we were able to share how we are feeling today by placing our sticks into a full, medium-filled, or almost empty bucket.

Then, the Bucket Squad brainstormed to create a list of ways to be bucket fillers in our school. One of the bucketfilling behaviors on our list is to greet people in confident and friendly ways. We learned that friendly greetings include smiling, looking people in the eye, and respecting personal space while using a kind tone of voice and appropriate volume. Wow, there is so much more to personal greetings than just saying hello!

Next, we learned about the Bucket Chart. All the kids received one to take to their classroom that they can either keep in their desks or another designated spot that the classroom teacher has chosen. The Bucket Chart is a great visual reminder to fill buckets with friendly greetings. Each time the kids use friendly greetings like the ones we practiced, they will be able to cross off a square on their Bucket Chart. This is also a wonderful way of seeing through concrete actions the relationship between how filling other people's buckets also helps us fill our own. The team should bring their Bucket Chart with them to our next group meeting.


Sincerely,



Your Name, Title_____

Phone: _____

Email: _____

**At Home Discussion:** Ask your child to show you examples of the friendly greetings we practiced. Discuss ways you can greet people and why this is an important life skill. You may also want to make a bucket at home to fill each time your child uses the learned bucketfilling skills.

# THE BUCKET SQUAD PLAYS CATCH
## Skill Learned
### Being a good listener fills buckets.

## OBJECTIVES:
**Participants will:**

⟩ Review friendly greetings

⟩ Discuss how being a bucket filler makes them feel about themselves

⟩ Learn listening skills

⟩ Practice listening attentively

## SUPPLIES NEEDED:

⟩ Group rules from Session One

⟩ Group buckets from Session One

⟩ Rolled paper strips, cotton balls, or other bucketfilling item

⟩ Check-in buckets and check-in sticks from Week Two

⟩ Balls (super balls, beach balls, or playground balls)

⟩ Bucket Chart

⟩ Letter for parents/teacher (Bucket Squad News)

## PREPARATION:
Before the group meeting, gather supplies and read through the curriculum. It is helpful to make several preparations prior to the group meeting. Here are a few suggestions:

**1.** Have the check-in buckets and check-in sticks out upon the students' arrival.

**2.** Have the Session One buckets out along with the filling item.

**3.** Copy the Bucket Chart and the Bucket Squad News. (One per Squad member.)

## GROUP CHECK IN: HOW FULL IS MY BUCKET? (10 minutes)
**PART 1:** Using the check-in buckets and craft sticks from Week Two, have group members check in. Sing the "How Are You?" song with younger kids.

**PART 2:** Give each student the individual bucket they made during Week One. Ask students to show you their Bucket Charts. Debrief about how giving friendly greetings impacted their week.

⟩ Did you notice yourself saying hello more often this past week?

⟩ Did you remember to use all parts of a friendly greeting? What are they?

⟩ Did you notice how this made the other person feel? How could you tell?

⟩ How did you feel when you made the extra effort to be especially friendly?

**PART 3:** Fill their buckets! To reinforce the concept that we feel good about ourselves when we are kind and respectful to others, distribute bucketfilling items to each group member. You can use rolled paper strips or you can choose pom-poms, cotton balls, marbles, foam stickers, or just about any other creative object you can imagine. Have the students place an item into their bucket for every square they checked off on their bucket chart. One way to make sure this does not become competitive is to focus on the collaborative effort of the group. Total the number of "X's" for the entire group. Then, focus on the impact the team made through their combined efforts to fill buckets!

> **Important:** It is okay if every square is crossed off. This first week was an easier goal and it is important that they feel success from the start. The bucket chart is an honor system. It is important to model trust to the kids. However, it is also okay to encourage honesty by explaining that being dishonest may cause guilty feelings. We wouldn't want them to dip into their own bucket in this way!

## OPENING ACTIVITY: (5 minutes)

Play a game called, "Seven's." Seat the students around a table. The leader starts this game by making a clapping pattern with her/his hands that consists of seven beats. For example, you can slap the table seven times or you can do a combination of clapping hands together, snapping, and slapping the table. You do the first seven beats and then the kids copy it. Then you add seven new beats using a different pattern. The kids try to copy both the first seven beats and the second seven beats. Then you add seven more beats. Typically, it works best if you start with an easy pattern and then progressively make it more difficult.

**Options:**

⍟ **K-2nd Grades:** You may want to play this game using less beats in a pattern.

⍟ **3rd-5th Grades:** You can let each group member add to the pattern.

## LEARNING ACTIVITIES: (20 minutes)

**Say to the group,** "Our game just introduced us to our bucketfilling goal for this week. If you were able to follow along during our game and picked up the patterns, you were using some important skills. Do you know what they were?"

**Hearing vs. Listening:** Hearing is simply noticing sounds, but when we are listening, we use our eyes, ears, body, and brain to process what we heard. Everyone must do their part to ensure that each person in the group can truly listen.

## Make the point!

Play a new game of "Seven's," but this time change the rules:

⍟ **Round 1:** Play with your eyes closed. How did this affect the success of the game?

⍟ **Round 2:** Make noise while playing the game by talking out loud, humming, or making some other audible distraction. How did this affect your success?

❧ **Round 3**: Turn away from the leader while playing the game. How did this affect the success of the game?

❧ **Round 4**: Do one last round with everyone using their eyes and ears, their bodies turned toward the leader, their thinking caps on, and cooperating. How did you feel playing the game this time? Was it less frustrating and more fun?

The leader says to the group, "We need to be good listeners to have good conversations with other people. If we make use of our eyes, ears, bodies and thinking caps, we make other people feel good because they know we are really listening! Listening also helps us know what kinds of questions we might want to ask someone who is speaking, and how to answer their questions. When we talk to other people and use good listening skills, it is a lot like playing a game of catch."

| Watching | Hearing | Body | Thinking Cap | Cooperation |
|---|---|---|---|---|
| *Using your eyes* | *Using your ears* | *Turned toward other person* | *Using your head* | *Working together toward a common goal* |

## Play catch with listening:
The group leader should demonstrate with a group member the following process:

**1.** Pair up group members.

**2.** Show the five ways we are good listeners:
   – Bodies facing one another
   – Eyes focused on each other
   – Ears tuned in to your partner and ready to hear
   – Thinking cap on
   – Being quiet so everyone can hear

**3.** Start by throwing the ball back and forth and learning the rhythm of playing catch. (One option for younger kids is to sit on the ground facing one another and roll the ball to each other.)

**4.** Now demonstrate playing catch with listening. Whoever has the ball is the one talking. The leader has the ball first and asks her/his partner a question, such as, "What is your favorite food?"

**5.** The partner then puts his hands out for the ball in order to answer the question, by saying, for example, "I like pizza."

**6.** The leader then puts out her/his hands to catch the ball and responds to her/his partner once having caught the ball again, "I love cheese pizza best. How about you?"

**7.** Demonstrate this until you think everyone understands how to play catch with listening.

**8.** Have the group members practice this with one another. Use the following sentence prompts as ideas. (One option: For each new sentence prompt, the kids could switch partners so they continue to interact with everyone.)

## Sentence Prompts:

⌇ What is your favorite summertime activity?

⌇ If you could be any animal, what would you be?

⌇ What foods do you least like?

⌇ If you could go anywhere on vacation, where would you go?

⌇ What is your favorite subject in school?
With older students, you may want to practice working on the skill of using follow up questions like, "Why?" Or, "What do/don't you like about that?"

## Discussion Points:

⌇ How could you tell your partner was listening to you?

⌇ Did you want to keep talking with your partner?

⌇ How did practicing listening help you come up with things to say?

⌇ How did you feel about yourself?

⌇ What would have happened if you were a "ball hog"? (Role-playing as a conversation hog is effective here!)

 Remind the kids that they normally will not be playing catch with a ball while having a conversation, but they can pretend they are by making sure that everyone is taking turns when talking.

## BUCKET CHART: (5 minutes)
### Weekly Goal: Fill buckets by playing catch with listening!

The Bucket Squad will be receiving a Bucket Chart to take with them again this week (see Appendix A). The team's goal for this week is to play catch with listening! They can cross off a square on their bucket chart each time they listen using their eyes, bodies, ears, and thinking caps while talking with another person. They should pretend that they are "playing catch." If a teacher or another adult notices the student using these skills, s/he can also cross off a square on the Bucket Chart. The team should bring the chart with them to the next Bucket Squad meeting. Remind the students that they should only mark a square if they are using all of the skills when listening that we practiced. Also tell them that the quality of the work is more important than the quantity. Ask the kids to pay attention to how the person they are listening to responds to them.

## CLOSING ACTIVITY: (3 minutes)
**K-1st Grade Option:** *The Bucket Squad Cheer!*

**2nd-5th Grade Option:** *The Bucket Squad Handshake!*

**Ask kids to pair up with a different partner this week to do the handshake!**
**Send home the Bucket Squad News.**

## CLASSROOM TIPS:

If you are using this curriculum to teach and reinforce bucketfilling in the classroom, here are a few tips to adjust this lesson:

Students enjoy the game of "Seven's" and it models the importance of listening to each other, but also highlights the way students should be listening during class lessons. Use the listening pictures to discuss the importance of our eyes, ears, bodies, and thinking caps when listening. The more often students practice the skills, the more actively engaged they will be in the classroom.

Throughout the week, the teacher can call on a pair of students to "play catch" with listening to continue to reinforce this bucketfilling behavior. You could also perform a role-play a day with the students. Another fun and unexpected listening game to play with your students is "Turn the tables on listening!" This is where you turn the tables by being a poor listener (interrupting or not letting your students speak). Then, ask the students how they felt when you weren't listening.

Explain to the students how they can fill their bucket this week. Keep working with the classroom system you implemented during week two. Edit the Bucket Squad News and share with parents or post information on your website.

# BUCKET SQUAD NEWS
## SESSION FOUR

**Dear Parent or Guardian:**

Today we started our meeting by playing a listening game. The leader of the game makes a pattern of beats using his or her hands. The leader can clap, slap the table, or snap. The rest of the group repeats the pattern. Then, the leader keeps adding to the pattern. We played the game by using our bodies. We turned toward the leader, our eyes watched, our ears heard the pattern, and our thinking caps helped us understand what we just heard so we could repeat it. After everyone got the hang of it, we all played with our eyes closed, and then with a lot of noise to distract us. This was one way to show the group that listening is so much more than hearing sounds. In order to be a good listener, everyone needs to cooperate. We also must use our bodies, eyes, ears, and thinking caps to give the person speaking our full attention.

After that, we had a chance to play a game of catch with listening! The group members paired up and threw a ball to one another while having a conversation. Only the person speaking could hold the ball. When it was the other person's turn to speak in the conversation, they received the ball from the speaker. This helped demonstrate that a conversation is two-sided. In other words, no one should be a "ball hog," or in this case, a conversation hog. It also illustrates the importance of turning toward the speaker, watching, hearing, and thinking about what was said.

The bucketfilling goal for this week is to listen attentively when having conversations with others. When the Bucket Squad uses their friendly greetings from last week in conjunction with being great listeners, they are bound to fill many buckets. In return, other people will notice how much fun it is to talk to them and may seek out more conversations with them, resulting in a fuller bucket for our Bucket Squad members as well.

Sincerely,


Your Name, Title_____

Phone: _____

Email: _____

 **At Home Discussion:** Ask your child to play catch with listening. They should also love to play the pattern game with you! Be sure to tell your child they are a bucket filler whenever you notice them being great listeners!

# WE LIKE THE BUCKET SQUAD
## Skill Learned
### Giving thoughtful compliments fills buckets.

## OBJECTIVES:
Participants will:
- Review listening
- Discuss how being a bucket filler makes them feel about themselves
- Learn how to give genuine compliments to others
- Practice giving good compliments
- Accept compliments appropriately

## SUPPLIES NEEDED:
- Group rules from Session One
- Group buckets from Session One
- Rolled paper strips, cotton balls, or other bucketfilling items
- Check-in buckets and check-in sticks from Session Two
- Tossing items (bean bags, small stuffed animals, or soft balls)
- Magazine photo of a non-famous person
- Photographs of Bucket Squad Members from Session One
- Colored paper
- Glue
- Pencils or markers
- Decorated chair
- Bucket Chart
- Letter for parents/teacher (Bucket Squad News)

## PREPARATION:
Before the group meeting, gather supplies and read through the curriculum. It is helpful to make several preparations prior to the group meeting. Here are a few suggestions:

**1.** Have the check-in buckets and check-in sticks out upon the students' arrival.

**2.** Have the Session One buckets available along with the filling item.

**3.** Copy the Bucket Chart and The Bucket Squad News for each member.

**4.** Decorate a special chair with balloons, crepe paper or a decorated sign.

# GROUP CHECK IN: HOW FULL IS MY BUCKET? (10 minutes)

**PART 1:** Using the check-in buckets and craft sticks from Week Two, have group members check in. Sing the "How Are You?" song with younger kids.

**PART 2:** Give each student the individual bucket they made during Week One. Ask students to show you their Bucket Charts. Discuss the results of playing catch with listening during this week.

⤳ Did you think about conversations like a game of catch?

⤳ How did it help?

⤳ What parts of your body did you use when you were listening?

⤳ What was difficult or challenging for you about listening?

⤳ What were you good at doing?

**PART 3:** Fill their buckets! To reinforce the concept that we feel good about ourselves when we show kindness and respect to others by listening, distribute bucketfilling items to each group member. Ask the students to place an item in their bucket for every square they checked off on their bucket chart. The Squad members will be adding to the items that are already in their buckets from last week. Whether a group member adds two items to their bucket or twenty, it is up to the leader to set a positive tone for all and celebrate each accomplishment. This will help ensure that the group members realize they are working together as a team.

> **Important:** It is okay if every square is crossed off. It shows in concrete actions that the more we fill other buckets, the fuller our own buckets become. The Bucket Chart is an honor system. It is important to model trust to the kids. However, it is also okay to encourage honesty by explaining that being dishonest may result in feelings of guilt or remorse. We wouldn't want them to dip into their own bucket in this way!

## OPENING ACTIVITY: (10 minutes)

### The Bucket Squad Compliment Toss!

Have group members stand in a large circle. The leader should have several tossing items (bean bags, small stuffed animals, or balls). The leader begins by choosing someone to whom s/he will toss the first bean bag. When the leader tosses it, s/he is to compliment the recipient. The leader illustrates this by saying, "I like your _____." The recipient catches the item and quickly says, "Thank you," while making eye contact with the thrower. Then, that person tosses the bean bag to a new person and gives a compliment starting with the same prompt, "I like your_____." After saying, "Thank you," that person throws the item to a new person, and so on. The game continues until everyone has had a turn and the item tossed is thrown back to the leader.

Now that the pattern has been established, play the game again. Follow the same pattern but change the sentence prompt. This time say, "I like the way you _____." Also, once the game has included a couple of players but isn't yet finished, the leader can start a new tossing game with another prompt while the current game is still ongoing. This time say, "I like it when you_____." The game continues in this manner with several items being tossed using the same pattern.

Practice the pattern once slowly. Then, add items and pick up the pace. See how quickly the group can get through the pattern and still throw out compliments.

For younger kids, it may be too difficult to have multiple tossing items going at the same time and you may want to play using just one compliment and tossing item at a time.

For older kids, you can make the game more challenging by adding this rule: Every time an item is dropped or someone forgets to give a compliment or say, "thank you," the game starts from the beginning.

## LEARNING ACTIVITIES: (30 minutes)

**Turning Compliments Inside-Out!:** Glue a photograph/magazine clipping of someone the kids do not know onto a piece of paper.

Ask the Bucket Squad, "What is a compliment?"

❧ **A compliment is when we say something nice to someone else.**

❧ **Some compliments focus on what is on the outside of a person, or what we can see.**
  • Looking at the photograph of the stranger, brainstorm to create a list of compliments that they can see.
  • Write them down on the paper on the outside of the photograph. Examples might be: "Nice eyes, cute hairstyle, I like her/his clothes, cool shoes, etc."
  • Why are these compliments easy to come up with even though you don't know the person?
  • Were most of the compliments in the opening game this kind of compliment? Why?

❧ **Other compliments focus on what kind of person or friend someone is.**
  • Using the Qualities List from Week Two, ask the kids whether or not they think any of those qualities belong to the person in the photo.
  • Why is it difficult to know whether they fit this individual? (Because you don't know what kind of person s/he is, what s/he likes to do for fun, or what s/he is good at doing.)

❧ **What are some compliments that people might give that show us that they know us from the inside-out?**
  • Brainstorm with the kids. Examples might be: "You are so nice. I like playing with you. You are so much fun. You make me laugh. You are smart at math. I like the way you share with me."

- Write down some of these ideas on the board or poster paper.

❧ **What is the difference between these compliments and why is that important?**
- When we receive a compliment about who we are on the inside, it lets us know that our friend has taken the time to get to know us and can name those attributes that make us the unique person we are. This kind of compliment creates a special feeling!
- Both kinds of compliments fill buckets, but this inside-out compliment goes a little further and puts more into a bucket at one time.
- Which kind of compliment would you rather receive from someone?

## Now let's compliment each other from the inside out!

**Say to the group**, "We have had five weeks to get to know one another. I want everyone to think of one compliment for each of the group members. Although there might be things you like about them on the outside, like their shirt or hair, your job is to come up with a compliment about who they are on the inside."

Instruct the group to:

**1.** Choose a piece of colored paper.

**2.** Glue your photograph onto the paper.

**3.** Write your name on the top of the paper.

The leader should:

❧ Choose a group member to begin the game and take that group member's paper.

❧ Tell the kids to really think about what they have learned about their group member. What do they like, admire, respect about her/him?

❧ Offer some examples of appropriate sentence prompts:
- I like the way you…
- You are really good at…
- One quality I've noticed about you is…

❧ Remind the students of what they learned previously about using eye contact and appropriate tone of voice, and the other learned communication skills.

❧ Have the first child sit in the specially decorated compliment chair.

❧ The leader should give a genuine compliment to the student first to illustrate how it should sound and look.

❧ Instruct the student in the chair that it's her/his job to smile and say, "Thank you," after a genuine compliment is given.

❧ Everyone else should take turns giving this student a genuine compliment.

❧ The leader can write the compliments down on the paper that has the child's photo attached to it.

❧ Repeat this until every student has had a turn!

## Discussion Points:

> How did it feel to give this kind of compliment?

> How did it feel to receive this kind of compliment?

> Was it hard to just say, "Thank you"?

> What happens to the compliment if you don't accept it? Does it still help to fill your bucket?

> Was it harder for you to give a compliment or to receive a compliment from someone else?

**Important:** By saying, "thank you," we are allowing others to fill our bucket. When we respond to compliments by saying, "That isn't true," or, "I am not," we are putting a lid on our bucket. It is important to graciously accept compliments and to feel good about it!

## BUCKET CHART: (5 minutes)

**Weekly Goal: Fill buckets by giving genuine compliments to others.**

Pass out a new Bucket Chart (see Appendix A) to the Bucket Squad members. The team's goal for this week is to give sincere compliments to other kids! They can cross off a square on their bucket chart each time they give someone a thoughtful compliment. They can cross off two squares for complimenting a friend on a quality or talent they like about them and one square for complimenting someone on the way they look. If a teacher catches the student using these skills, s/he can also cross off a square on the Bucket Chart. The team should bring the chart with them to the next Bucket Squad meeting.

*Learn how to give genuine compliments to others and practice giving good compliments*

## CLOSING ACTIVITY: (3 minutes)

**K-1st Grade Option:** *The Bucket Squad Cheer!*

**2nd-5th Grade Option:** *The Bucket Squad Handshake!*

{ **Ask kids to pair up with a different partner this week to do the handshake!**
**Send home the Bucket Squad News.** }

# CLASSROOM TIPS:

If you are implementing this curriculum to teach and reinforce bucketfilling in the classroom, here are a few tips to adjust this lesson:

Spending a week on learning about how to give and receive genuine compliments is an important investment in your students' lives. This skill is a basic building block in all relationships and the small group lesson can be easily adjusted for a classroom setting.

The activity with a photograph/magazine clipping of someone the students do not know can be done by a large group or, depending on the age of your students, this could be a great opportunity for small group work as well.

The lesson of the compliment chair could be a learning tool that you utilize throughout the week. It might be a great way to both start and end your school day, making sure that each student has a turn in the compliment chair at some point during the week. Another option is to use photos of each child and attach them to a sheet of paper. Have the class write compliments on each student's paper during a class activity.

*Practicing giving good compliments is vital, but it is equally important to practice receiving compliments.*

Practicing giving good compliments is vital, but it is equally important to practice receiving compliments. If students are older, you can lead a discussion about why sometimes it is difficult to take a compliment from others due to peer pressure or insecurities. But, if we don't take the compliment, we are not allowing our bucket to fill and we are denying the person giving the compliment the result of that act, which are their good feelings. So, when students are in the compliment chair, encourage them to smile and say thank you when they receive a compliment from a classmate.

Using the system you developed earlier, keep track as a class on the compliments that the children give in your classroom. Reinforce this by filling your classroom bucket. Confirm that students are noting how they feel on the inside when they give genuine compliments to others.

Please be sure to review the idea that their using friendly greetings and good listening skills is still being observed and acknowledged by you, too. Take time to praise kids who are working hard to continue using the first two bucketfilling behaviors.

If your students are being friendly, listening intently and giving compliments, how full is your bucket? Hopefully, you are paying attention to how the classroom experiences are affecting you as well.

Finally, adapt the Bucket Squad News for week five and update your parents by sending home a newsletter or posting to your classroom website.

# BUCKET SQUAD NEWS
## SESSION FIVE

**Dear Parent or Guardian:**

Our opening game was a lot of fun today. We played a game called The Bucket Squad Compliment Toss! We stood in a circle and threw a soft item in a pattern. When we threw the item, we gave a compliment to the person catching it. That person had to quickly say, "Thank you," and then throw the item to the next person with a compliment. It was exciting to see how many items we could use in the pattern, and how many compliments the students received.

Next, we talked about the difference between complimenting someone on what we can see outside versus praising something we like about them on the inside. For example, the compliment, "I like your shirt," is different from, "I like how you share with me." Then, we practiced giving genuine compliments. Each group member sat in a special compliment chair. We each came up with one sincere compliment to say to that person. The compliments people said were written down on a piece of paper for each child to keep.

Another important lesson we learned about compliments is the importance of responding by saying, "Thank you." If we refuse a compliment, it is like preventing our own buckets from being filled.

The bucketfilling goal for this week is to give compliments to others. When we take the time to think of a compliment about someone on the inside, we will cross off two squares on our chart. For a compliment about how someone looks on the outside, we will cross off one square on our chart. Compliments are quick and easy ways to fill other people's buckets. But the more sincere the compliment is, the better they make both the recipient and the giver feel.

Sincerely,

Your Name, Title_____

Phone: _____

Email: _____

**At Home Discussion:** Ask your child to show you the compliment page they received today. Practice giving sincere compliments to everyone in your family during dinner.

## THE BUCKET SQUAD LEARNS TEAMWORK
### Skill Learned
Sharing and taking turns fills buckets.

## OBJECTIVES:
Participants will:
- ⊘ Review giving and receiving genuine compliments
- ⊘ Learn about cooperation and sharing
- ⊘ Practice by working together

## SUPPLIES NEEDED:
Group rules from Session One
- ⊘ Group buckets from Session One
- ⊘ Check-in buckets and check-in sticks from Session Two
- ⊘ 24-piece puzzles or Maze (made from tape)
- ⊘ Markers
- ⊘ Bucket Chart

## PREPARATION:
Before the group meeting, gather supplies and read through the curriculum. It is helpful to make several preparations prior to the group meeting. Here are a few suggestions:

**I.** Have the check-in buckets and check-in sticks out upon the students' arrival each week.

**2.** Divide puzzle pieces into baggies (K-2).

**3.** Create the maze ahead of time (3-5).

**4.** Make copies of bucket chart for each group member.

## GROUP CHECK IN: (5 to 10 minutes)
### How Full Is My Bucket?

**PART I:** Using the check-in buckets and craft sticks from Session Two, have group members check-in. Sing the "How Are You?" song with younger kids.

**PART 2:** Give each student the individual bucket they made from Session One. Ask students to show you their Bucket Charts. Discuss the results of giving and receiving compliments during the past week.

- ⊘ Tell me some examples of compliments you gave people last week.

- ⊘ Did you give a compliment to someone you don't often see?

- ⊘ How about at home? Did you compliment anyone in your family this week?

⍟ What did you notice when you gave people compliments?

⍟ How did you feel?

⍟ Did others compliment you?

**PART 3:** Fill their buckets! To reinforce the concept that we feel good about ourselves when we genuinely compliment other people, distribute bucketfilling items to each group member. Ask the students to place an item in their bucket for every square they checked off on their bucket chart. The Squad members will be adding to the items that are already in their buckets from last week. Whether a group member adds two items to their bucket or twenty, it is up to the leader to set a positive tone and celebrate each accomplishment. This will help ensure that the group members realize they are working together as a team.

**Important:** It is okay if every square is crossed off. It shows in concrete actions that the more we fill other buckets, the fuller our own buckets become. The Bucket Chart is an honor system. It is important to model trust to the kids. However, it is also okay to encourage honesty by explaining that being dishonest may result in feelings of guilt or remorse. We wouldn't want them to dip into their own bucket in this way!

## OPENING ACTIVITY: (5 minutes)

### The Bucket Squad Would Rather...

Group members should stand up for this game. Tell the students that you are going to give the group members two choices. There is no right or wrong answer, but they do need to pick one of the choices. They will not be talking. To demonstrate their response, they will walk to one side of the room for choice A and the other side of the room for choice B. (If you don't have room to walk, you can have them stand for A and sit for B). As you play this game, you will gradually take the questions from fun and light-hearted to prompts that will help you discuss the topics of getting along with others and teamwork.

### Possible Sentence Prompts:

Would you rather...

Ⓐ Play in the snow **or**    Ⓑ Swim at the beach?

Ⓐ Sleep in a tent   **or**    Ⓑ Stay in a hotel?

Ⓐ Watch television **or**    Ⓑ Read a book?

Ⓐ Stay up late     **or**    Ⓑ Go to bed early?

Ⓐ Ride a bike      **or**    Ⓑ Ride a scooter?

Ⓐ Eat vanilla **or** Ⓑ Chocolate ice cream?

Ⓐ Play with a group **or** Ⓑ With just one friend at a time?

Ⓐ Be told what to do **or** Ⓑ Take turns leading?

Ⓐ Give a compliment **or** Ⓑ Receive a compliment?

## LEARNING ACTIVITIES: (30 minutes)

### Cooperation and Teamwork!

**K-2nd Grade:** Divide the pieces of a 24-piece puzzle ahead of time into equal portions in baggies. Give each child their own baggie.

Tell the students that they are going to put a puzzle together today as a group. Each of them has important pieces to the puzzle and they will need to work together to make the picture complete.

### Rules of the game:

**1.** Everyone lays out their pieces face up in front of them.

**2.** The leader keeps one piece in the center.

**3.** Kids can try to fit their own pieces together or try matching them to the piece in the center.

**4.** The students cannot take a piece from anyone else. However, they can offer one or more pieces to someone else if they work in a certain part of the puzzle the other child possesses.

**5.** Play continues until the puzzle is complete.

### Questions for Discussion:

⬙ Did everyone have a part in putting the puzzle together?

⬙ Why do you think you were not allowed to take a piece from someone else?

⬙ Was sharing involved in this game?

⬙ What would have happened if one person took over the game?

⬙ Do you think the puzzle was completed faster by the classmates working together?

⬙ Was this a fair way to play?

⬙ Why did the game have rules?

⬙ How do rules help us to play fair?

⬙ What kinds of games do you play while at recess with your friends? How can you make those games fair and give everyone a turn?

**3rd – 5th Grade:** Create a maze for students to learn teamwork. You can either create a grid on the floor with masking tape or place duct tape on a tarp you can purchase from a home improvement store.

## Sample Maze

| X<br>6<br>Finish | | | |
|---|---|---|---|
| | X<br>Step<br>5 | X<br>Step<br>4 | |
| | | X<br>Step<br>3 | |
| | X<br>Step<br>2 | | |
| X<br>1<br>Start | | | |

## Rules of the Game:

**1.** Teach the kids that the object of the game is to find the correct path through the maze. This is a team game, and no one is the winner until they all win by getting through the maze successfully.

**2.** Line up all the kids at the end of the maze. The steps are not labeled on the maze, only the group leader knows the correct steps through the maze.

**3.** There is **no talking** during this game.

**4.** The first child in line chooses one of the 4 squares in the first row for the first step. If the square is the right one, the leader says yes, nods her head or rings a bell. If the square is not the correct one, the leader says no, shakes her head or uses a buzzer.

**5.** If the child chose the correct one, then he can try to find step 2. The child can move left, right, forward or diagonally, but never backward. The child's turn continues until he chooses an incorrect step. Then that child goes to the back of the line.

**6.** The next child in line takes his/her turn. If she was watching, she will know which squares not to try based on the previous child's decisions. If the previous child made any right choices, this next participant will know how to start and then try a new square. This child also goes to the back of the line when she steps on an incorrect square.

**7.** The next child will try and this turn-taking continues until one child makes it completely through the maze.

**8.** The game is not over until everyone on the team successfully navigates through the maze.

## Discussion Questions:

🔖 What worked during this game?

🔖 What was difficult during this game? (Usually the kids bring up the challenge of not talking.)

🔖 Why do you think there was a no talking rule during this game? (So no one could take over and control the game. The rule also made it difficult to argue.)

🔖 Since you couldn't talk, what else helped you to work together as a team? (Paying attention to the other players, pointing to the right square or showing a teammate where to go when he needed help.)

🔖 Once kids realize that they can still communicate even without words, they often want to play the game a second time. Come up with a new "right way" through the maze.

🔖 Let them play again if time allows.

🔖 How did you work together to get through the maze a second time?

🔖 In what ways did you communicate with each other this time?

🔖 In what ways do we communicate with our classmates, teachers, or family every day without words? (By eye-rolling, smiling, frowning, glaring, including or excluding others.)

🔖 Why is it important to be aware of how we communicate with and without words? How does this help us be a good classmate and teammate?

## BUCKET CHART: (5 Minutes)

**Weekly Goal: Fill buckets by cooperating and sharing with others.**

Pass out a new Bucket Chart (see Appendix A) to the Bucket Squad members. The team's goal for this week is to take turns and share with others in the school. Examples of this might be playing what someone else wants to play on the playground, and taking turns, sharing or working together on a project in the classroom. They can cross off a square on their bucket chart for cooperating with others. If a teacher catches the student using these skills, he or she can also cross off a square on the Bucket Chart. The team should bring the chart with them to the next Bucket Squad meeting.

## CLOSING ACTIVITY: (3 minutes)
**K-1st Grade Option:** *The Bucket Squad Cheer!*

**2nd-5th Grade Option:** *The Bucket Squad Handshake!*

{ **Ask kids to pair up with a different partner this week to do the handshake!** }
**Send home the Bucket Squad News.**

## CLASSROOM TIPS:

If you are using this curriculum to teach and reinforce bucketfilling in the classroom, here are a few tips to adjust this lesson:

If you choose to do these teamwork activities in the classroom, it is best to have several sets of 24-piece puzzles. Divide the students into small groups and give each group a puzzle to put together following the instructions and rules listed in the outline. Then you can discuss the activity with the whole class.

For students in older grades, the maze also works great as a large group activity, but I usually divide the students into two large groups and have two separate mazes so students have more opportunities to participate. It can also be fun to encourage a friendly competition between the two teams. You can still conduct the discussion with the entire class.

Make it a classroom goal to cooperate, work together, and share together this week. Keep track of your students' efforts by continuing the classroom bucket chart.

Taking turns, working together, cooperating and sharing Fills Buckets!

# BUCKET SQUAD NEWS
## SESSION SIX

**Dear Parent or Guardian:**

After playing the game "Would You Rather?" the Bucket Squad learned about teamwork by using cooperation.

Students either worked as a group to put a puzzle together or they helped each other walk through a maze. Both games had special rules that encouraged cooperation and teamwork. Ask your child to tell you which game s/he played and what s/he learned from it. After the game, the children identified what helped them work together with others, such as including everyone, obeying the rules to be fair, and taking turns. We also discussed how cooperation fills buckets, but being bossy or arguing over games tends to empty buckets.

The group's goal for this week is to use cooperation by sharing and taking turns with others. Every time they do this, they can cross off a square on their bucket chart! This should be a fun week for them and their classmates!


Sincerely,


Your Name, Title_____

Phone: _____

Email: _____


**At Home Discussion:** Were their cooperation skills modeled at home this week? Have a discussion with your child about how families need to work together too. How does cooperation affect everyone's bucket in the family?

## THE BUCKET SQUAD SOLVES PROBLEMS
### Skill Learned

How to use an "It Dips" statement to protect my bucket when someone dips into my bucket.

## OBJECTIVES:

❧ Participants will:

❧ Review working together, cooperating, and sharing

❧ Learn how to use an "It Dips" statement and why it works to help solve problems.

❧ Practice using "It Dips" statements.

## SUPPLIES NEEDED:

❧ Group rules from Session One

❧ Group buckets from Session One

❧ Check-in buckets and check-in sticks from Session Two

❧ Feeling charades cards

❧ Feeling charades answer sheet

❧ Feelings poster (if you have one)

❧ Markers

❧ Bucket Chart

## PREPARATION:

Before the group meeting, gather supplies and read through the curriculum. It is helpful to make several preparations prior to the group meeting. Here are a few suggestions:

**1.** Have the check-in buckets and check-in sticks out upon the students' arrival each week.

**2.** Cut out the feeling charades cards beforehand.

**3.** Copy a feeling charades answer sheet to give to each group member.

**4.** Copy the bucket chart to give to each group member.

## GROUP CHECK IN: (5 to 10 minutes)

### How Full Is My Bucket?

**PART 1:** Using the check-in buckets and craft sticks from Session Two, have group members check-in. Sing the "How Are You?" song with younger kids.

**PART 2:** Give each student the individual bucket they made from Session One. Ask students to show you their Bucket Charts. Discuss the results of working together, taking turns, and sharing to learn if these skills benefited them during the past week.

⚝ Name one time you worked together with a group of kids on the playground or in your neighborhood.

⚝ Was it ever hard to cooperate? What was difficult about it?

⚝ How do you think your friends felt when you worked together with them?

⚝ How did you feel?

⚝ Did you notice whether or not it helped you get along better with others?

**PART 3:** Fill their buckets! To reinforce the concept that we feel good about ourselves when we work together, cooperate and share with others, distribute bucketfilling items to each group member. Have the students place an item into their bucket for every square they checked off on their bucket chart. The Squad members will be adding to the items that are already in their buckets from last week. Whether a group member adds two items to their bucket or twenty, it is up to the leader to set a positive tone and celebrate each accomplishment. This will help ensure that the group members realize they are working together as a team.

**Important:** It is okay if every square is crossed off. It shows in concrete actions that the more we fill other buckets, the fuller our own buckets become. The Bucket Chart is an honor system. It is important to model trust to the kids. However, it is also okay to encourage honesty by explaining that being dishonest may result in feelings of guilt or remorse. We wouldn't want them to dip into their own bucket in this way!

## OPENING ACTIVITY: (15 minutes)

### Feeling Charades

To start group this week, play a game of feeling charades.

**1.** Cut apart the feeling chart on page 58 to make feeling cards.

**2.** Turn the cards over and place them in the middle of the group.

**3.** Give every person a feeling charades answer sheet (p.59) and pencil.

**4.** Choose a fair way to start the game (such as youngest player goes first). The player draws a card. Then, they must act out the card using only their body and facial expressions. They cannot use words.

**5.** The rest of the players guess what feeling the student is showing by writing their answer on their paper. If you have a feelings poster, it could be helpful to the group (especially younger kids) to hang it in the room as a reference. You can also compose a list of feelings words before the class begins.

**6.** Make a t-chart on a whiteboard or a piece of tag board. The t-chart has two categories, match and mismatch.

**7.** After acting out a feeling for the students to identify, and when everyone has written down their answer, go around the room and ask each player what feeling s/he wrote down.

**8.** Keep a tally of how many feelings match and how many feelings mismatch as you play the game.

**9.** Play continues until everyone has had a turn.

## Discussion Questions:

🖋 Were some feelings easier to guess than others?

🖋 Which feelings looked the same?

🖋 Why do you think there were mismatches?

🖋 If we had been able to use words while playing the game, do you think it would have been easier? Why or why not?

🖋 What do you think we can learn from this game?

**Say to the group:** "We all have feelings but sometimes it is hard to know the right feeling word. This game shows how easily misunderstandings can happen between friends. Sometimes we think we know how someone feels but we don't. Other times, people may not even know their exact feeling but they know they feel bad or upset. This usually means that our buckets have been dipped into. Because it can be hard to find the words to describe our emotions, people often say hurtful things in these situations or just don't talk to each other at all, both of which can make the problem worse. But using an "It dips" message can make it easy to find words that help us to solve problems without dipping into someone else's bucket and causing the problem to grow."

*Sometimes we think we know how someone feels but we don't, other times, people may not even know their exact feeling but they know they feel bad or upset,*

# FEELING CHARADES CARDS

| | | |
|---|---|---|
| Happy | Angry | Surprised |
| Scared | Nervous | Annoyed |
| Bored | Worried | Excited |
| Frustrated | Jealous | Lonely/<br>Left out |

# FEELING CHARADES ANSWER SHEET

Write down a feeling you think your group member is showing you.

| Group Member Name | I think s/he is feeling... | S/he is really feeling... |
|---|---|---|
| 1. | | |
| 2. | | |
| 3. | | |
| 4. | | |
| 5. | | |
| 6. | | |
| 7. | | |
| 8. | | |

How many matches did you get? _____

How many mismatches do you have?_____

# LEARNING ACTIVITIES: "It dips" are the magic words! (20 minutes)

Take a volunteer student aside and plan out a role play so that s/he knows what to do. Have her/him pretend that you are both lining up for lunch. The student volunteer should cut in front of you in line.

**ACT 1:** Say to the student, "You cut in line!" The student should defend her/himself by saying, "No I didn't. I was here first!" You can continue this by getting into a pretend argument, which can happen when our buckets get dipped because we have an urge to dip back. The skit can end with someone calling the other one a name or telling a teacher.

Discuss with the group: Did bucket dipping happen in this skit? Who dipped into whose bucket first? Did the other person's bucket also get dipped? How? How did each person feel at the end? Did two wrongs make a right? Was the problem solved or were both kids' feelings hurt?

Now, watch the same situation but notice the change in words…

**ACT 2:** Have the student cut in front of you in line again. But this time say to the student, **"It dips my bucket when you cut in front of me in line."** Let the student who is role-playing with you respond. S/he will likely respond with less anger than in the first role-play and will probably apologize and move. It is important to say the "It dips" message without sounding angry. You can demonstrate this importance by re-running the scene and using the same words, but this time with an angry voice.

## Learning the 3 parts to the "It Dips" Message:

**1.** "It dips my bucket…" or "That dipped my bucket."
This statement tells someone they caused you to feel hurt. Sometimes that is all you need to say and the other person will either recognize what they did and say they are sorry, or they may ask you, "What dipped your bucket?

**2.** When you_____
(Tell the person what they are doing that you do not like.) The person may then try to make it right. If they don't apologize or change the situation, you can ask them to help make it right by using step 3.

**3.** I want_____
(Tell the person what you want them to do to make it right.)

## Practice:

Use the following situations to practice using the "It Dips" statement. A variety of prompts are listed below. Some will be better for younger kids and others for the older. Most of the situations display a possible conflict, but a couple of them are positive situations. It is important to let the kids know that "It" messages can be used to show someone appreciation and express positive feelings as well, by changing the message from "It Dips" to "It Fills." Read the situation out loud and ask students to come up with possible ways to respond using the parts of an "It Dips" or "It Fills" statement. Discuss the different options they selected. Then, have the group members pair up and practice saying the "It Dips" message to their partner. When they do this, they should be careful to say the words calmly but firmly and look their partner directly in the eye while they say it. It is important to show confidence so the other person takes them seriously.

## Younger students:

- You ask to join a game at recess and someone tells you no.
- Your friend won't share a toy with you.
- A friend asks you to play but doesn't want your other friend to play with the two of you.
- A classmate tells you that they don't like the picture you drew.
- A friend escorts you to the school nurse when you get hurt.

## Older students:

- You are working with a group to come up with ideas for a project and it doesn't seem like anyone is listening to your ideas.
- You heard that someone is spreading a rumor about you.
- Your friends are being mean to someone and you know that what they are doing isn't right.
- One of your friends isn't hanging out with you anymore and you aren't sure why.
- A friend tells you congratulations when you were selected for a team and he wasn't.

## BUCKET CHART: (5 minutes)

**Weekly Goal: Use "It Dips"/Fills" Messages this week to protect your bucket and to fill others.**

Pass out a new Bucket Chart (see Appendix A) to the Bucket Squad members. The team's goal for this week is to use "It Dips" or "It Fills" statements to tell other people when they got hurt or when somebody did something nice for them. They can cross off a square on their bucket chart for using "It Dips" to problem solve or "It Fills" to express gratitude. If a teacher catches the student using these skills, s/he can also cross off a square on the Bucket Chart. The team should bring the chart with them to the next Bucket Squad meeting.

## CLOSING ACTIVITY: (3 minutes)

**K-1st Grade Option:** *The Bucket Squad Cheer!*

**2nd-5th Grade Option:** *The Bucket Squad Handshake!*

**Ask kids to pair up with a different partner this week to do the handshake!**

**Send home the Bucket Squad News.**

## CLASSROOM TIPS:

If you are using this curriculum to teach and reinforce bucketfilling in the classroom, here are a few tips to adjust this lesson:

This lesson is easily adapted to the classroom. The feeling charades activity can be played in a couple of different ways. One way is to draw several names and have those students be the actors while the rest of the students can be the guessers. Or you could make several sets of cards and place the kids in small groups so several games are going at the same time. Then, you can have a class discussion to talk about the importance of using words, along with using body language to express oneself. You can also talk about how sometimes when we are feeling very emotional, it is difficult to find a feeling word to express that emotion accurately.

Sometimes when we are feeling very emotional, it is difficult to find a feeling word to express that emotion accurately.

Demonstrating and practicing the "It Dips" or "It Fills" statements can be modeled to the entire class. Then, pair up the students. Read the selected situations out loud and ask the groups to practice with one another. Afterward, call on a few pairs to demonstrate for the class what they learned.

Throughout the week, you might start each day reviewing "It Dips" statements. Ask the class if they have an example of using one that they would like to share. When there are conflicts in the classroom, encourage the students to use "It Dips" messages for problem solving. You can also discuss the use of "It Dips" messages while reading to the class. Literature is full of conflicts that are not solved well or led to arguments. Stop the class during those places in the story and ask the students what would have been different in the resolution of conflict if the character had used an "It Dips" statement. What could the character have said? How might it have changed the story?

Make it a classroom goal to use "It Dips" or "It Fills" statements. Keep track of your students' efforts by continuing the use of the classroom bucket chart.

# BUCKET SQUAD NEWS
## SESSION SEVEN

**Dear Parent or Guardian:**

After reviewing the importance of cooperating and team work, we played a game of feelings charades. The kids took turns acting out a feeling without words. Then we had a discussion about how certain feelings can look the same. For example, it can be difficult to know if someone is feeling frustrated or angry. Sometimes it is hard for even us to know exactly how we are feeling, especially when we are upset. This is why we shouldn't expect or assume that our friends know how we feel just by the way we are acting. However, when we do tell them our feelings, it is important to do so without bucket dipping. So, today we learned how to use "It Dips" statements.

"It Dips" messages allow the kids to tell their peers that they are hurt even if they can't find the exact feeling word. It also allows them to state what they need to feel better in a calm and respectful way. The 3 parts are listed below along with some examples:

Part 1: It dips my bucket_____

Part 2: When_____

Part 3: I want_____

"It dips my bucket when you don't let me play; I want to play the game too."
"It dips my bucket when you take my markers; I want you to ask."

The students practiced coming up with "It Dips" statements for varying situations. Then they said the "It Dips" message to a partner. The Bucket Squad can cross off a square on their bucket chart each time they use an "It Dips" message this week. This is a great way to keep from dipping into other people's buckets, but more importantly, it protects our own good feelings in our buckets. An "It Dips" statement is like putting a lid on the bucket because it helps the kids stand up for themselves in a respectful and proactive way.

Sincerely,

Your Name, Title_____

Phone: _____

Email: _____

{ **At Home Discussion:** Practice using "It Dips" messages at home this week. }

## THE BUCKET SQUAD DETECTIVES
### Skill Learned

Identifying clues that someone's bucket needs filling. when someone dips into my bucket.

## OBJECTIVES:

- Participants will:
- Review giving "It Dips" or "It Fills" statements
- Learn about being a bucket detective
- Practice being a bucket detective

## SUPPLIES NEEDED:

- Group rules from Session One
- Group buckets from Session One
- Check-in buckets and check-in sticks from Session Two
- Spy glass worksheet
- Random act scenarios
- Markers
- Bucket Chart

## PREPARATION:

Before the group meeting, gather supplies and read through the curriculum. It is helpful to make several preparations prior to the group meeting. Here are a few suggestions:

1. Have the check-in buckets and check-in sticks out upon the students' arrival each week.
2. Choose which "I Spy" game you are going to play. If using the tray game, prepare the tray ahead of time.
3. Copy the spyglass worksheet for each group member (K-2nd grades).
4. Copy the TV/movie character worksheet for each group member (3rd-5th grades).
5. Copy the bucket chart for each group member.

## GROUP CHECK IN: (5 to 10 minutes)
### How Full Is My Bucket?

**PART 1:** Using the check-in buckets and craft sticks from Session Two, have group members check-in. Sing the "How Are You?" song with younger kids.

**PART 2:** Give each student their individual bucket from Session One. Ask students to show you their Bucket Charts. Discuss how using "It Dips" messages worked for the group.

- How many times did you use an "It Dips" message this week?
- Give an example of the situation and what you said.
- How did it work?
- Were you able to solve problems better?
- Was there anything that was hard about it?
- Does anyone want to act one out today?

**PART 3:** Fill their buckets! To reinforce the concept that we protect our buckets when we use "It Dips" statements to problem solve, distribute bucketfilling items to each group member. Have the students place an item into their bucket for every square they checked off on their bucket chart. If they kept track of using "It Fills" messages, they can also put items in their bucket for that. The Squad members will be adding to the items that are already in their buckets from previous weeks. Whether a group member adds two items to their bucket or twenty, it is up to the leader to set a positive tone and celebrate each accomplishment. This will help ensure that the group members realize they are working together as a team

> **Important:** It is okay if every square is crossed off. It shows in concrete actions that the more we fill other buckets, the fuller our own buckets become. The Bucket Chart is an honor system. It is important to model trust to the kids. However, it is also okay to encourage honesty by explaining that being dishonest may result in feelings of guilt or remorse. We wouldn't want them to dip into their own bucket in this way!

## OPENING ACTIVITY: (10 minutes)
### Play a quick game of "I spy…"
To introduce the topic this week, play a game that requires students to use observation and critical thinking skills to detect what is missing. Here are a couple of options:

**K - 2nd Grades Option:**
**Tray Game:** Place several small objects on a tray. Objects might include a ball, eraser, pencil, crayons, a card, etc.  You can either keep the tray in another part of the room or cover the tray with a cloth or paper so the students cannot view the objects on the tray. Tell the students that you will allow them 10 seconds to look at what is on the tray. Then walk away with the tray and take an item off the tray. Show the students the tray again and see if they can "spy" what is missing. You can also add something to the tray. Repeat this several times, with different items.

**3rd - 5th Grades:**
**What's different about me?** In this game, one person goes out into the hall and changes something about their appearance. They could put their hair into a ponytail or take off the band holding a ponytail, they might take out an earring, or roll up their pant legs. The group leader can be the one to go into the hall and make changes or have the group members take turns being "it." When the student returns to the room, everyone else must try to "spy" the change.

**Discuss with the Bucket Squad:**

꙲ Was the game difficult at the beginning?

꙲ Was the game easier toward the end?

꙲ What does a detective do?

꙲ In what way was this game like being a detective?

꙲ What helped you to detect what was different? (Observing, paying attention to details, practicing.)

## LEARNING ACTIVITIES: Bucket Detectives! (30 minutes)

**Say to the group,** "Even though everyone's bucket is invisible, people give a lot of hints about how full or empty their buckets are. What does it mean to have a full bucket? How might you know just by looking at someone that their bucket is probably pretty full? Think like a detective. What kind of clues can you find?

Brainstorm with the kids:

꙲ Smiling

꙲ Laughing

꙲ Standing tall

꙲ Looking friendly

꙲ Working hard

꙲ Getting along well with others

꙲ Is included or includes others

What does it mean to have an empty bucket? How could you tell by looking at someone that their bucket might be almost empty? Think like a detective. What kind of clues can you find? Think about how someone with an empty bucket might look or act.

꙲ Sad

꙲ Angry

꙲ Lonely

꙲ Teasing others or is being teased by others

꙲ Is being left out/not included

**Leader says to the group:** "Since we are the bucket squad, what do you think we should do if we use our detective skills and notice someone who seems to have an empty bucket? That's right… WE SHOULD FILL IT!"

**K-2nd Grade Option:**

**Make a spyglass:** Students love pretending they are a real detective. The following page has a spyglass worksheet you can use for this project.

 You can occasionally find inexpensive spy glasses at a dollar or discount store as well. It can be fun for the kids to act out this activity with a real spyglass!

## Directions:

**1.** Copy the spyglass onto cardstock and cut out.

**2.** Then, cut out the word CLUES. Glue the word CLUES to the front of the spyglass.

**3.** Find the words and pictures on this page that are hints that someone's bucket might need filling. Cut those words and pictures out and glue them onto the spyglass around the word CLUES.

**4.** Cut out the word ACTIONS and glue it to the back side of the spyglass.

**5.** Cut out the words and pictures that describe ways to help fill a bucket and glue them around the word ACTIONS.

**6.** Keep your spyglass handy to help you remember how to be a BUCKET DETECTIVE!

Hurt

Ask for Help

Sad

Friendly

Listen

Angry

Scared

Take Turns

Being Teased

**3rd -5th Grade Option:**

**How full is your favorite TV character's bucket?**

**Directions:** Have the students practice being bucket detectives by participating in the following activity.

**1.** As a group, brainstorm to create a list of popular television shows or movies.

**2.** Choose a television show or movie for the group to use as practice for being bucket detectives.

**3.** Pass out the worksheet on page 70. You can either go through the worksheet together as a group or ask the kids to work as partners.

**4.** Finally, use the discussion points below to talk about the worksheet.

> **Option:** You can choose a TV show or movie ahead of time that will offer great examples of characters and buckets. You could even show a clip of the show or movie.

## Worksheet Discussion Points:

⏿ Do the characters' bucket levels change during the show?

⏿ Is there anyone who is a bucket filler on the show? How do you know?

⏿ Is there anyone who is a bucket dipper? How do you know?

⏿ Is there a relationship between the way they treat other people and how full their own bucket is?

⏿ What clues do they give about their buckets?

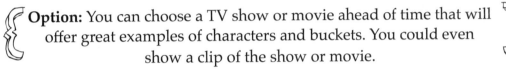

Even though everyone's bucket is invisible, people give a lot of hints about how full or empty their buckets are.

**Say to the group,** "Your classmates give hints about their buckets too. Now that you have practiced being a bucket detective by thinking about this TV show / movie, you will be a better bucket detective with your friends."

# Title of TV Show or Movie

| Character's Name | Bucket filler? Or Bucket dipper? | How full is the character's bucket? Empty, So-So, or Full | How do you know? What clues does the character give? |
| --- | --- | --- | --- |
|  |  |  |  |
|  |  |  |  |
|  |  |  |  |
|  |  |  |  |

# BUCKET CHART: (5 minutes)

**Weekly Goal: Be a detective and look for kids who need you to fill their buckets!**

Pass out a new Bucket Chart (see Appendix A) to the Bucket Squad members. The team's goal for this week is to be on the lookout for kids who might need a friend. When they find someone who looks sad, lonely, left out or upset, they can use the bucketfilling skills they have been practicing to fill others' buckets. It is up to them how they fill it. They can choose from the bucketfilling strategies they have learned. They can cross off a square on their bucket chart each time they find someone who could benefit from bucketfilling. If a teacher catches the student using these skills, s/he can also cross off a square on the Bucket Chart. The team should bring the chart with them to the next Bucket Squad meeting.

# CLOSING ACTIVITY: (3 minutes)

**K-1st Grade Option:** *The Bucket Squad Cheer!*

**2nd-5th Grade Option:** *The Bucket Squad Handshake!*

**Ask kids to pair up with a different partner this week to do the handshake!**
**Send home the Bucket Squad News.**

 # CLASSROOM TIPS:

If you are using this curriculum to teach and reinforce bucketfilling in the classroom, here are a few tips to adjust the weekly lesson:

This is a fun lesson to do as a class. Playing "I spy" can be easily adapted to the classroom setting and is a great way to introduce the idea of paying attention to detail the way a detective has to pay attention to clues. You can play either the 'tray game' or the 'what's different about me' game as a whole class, or you can break up into small groups. You can play the game once daily for a week.

Both of the worksheets can also be utilized in the classroom setting without much modification. The spyglass worksheet can easily be taught with whole class instruction, allowing time for the kids to cut, paste and complete the worksheet. The TV character worksheet is a great way to have a class discussion about bucketfilling, bucket dipping and the choices we make each day about how we treat others. This can also be a great time to talk about the word reputation and how reputations are formed. What are the reputations of the characters in the television show? Watching an episode or showing a clip from a television show that you discuss can be helpful.

Remind your students that they have been working on many ways to be a bucket filler over the past several weeks. But, you can also remind them, it is equally important to notice when other kids might need their buckets filled. This continues to build empathy and helps students to make more friends. After all, to have a friend, we need to be a friend!

Have students keep track of how many times they spy an empty bucket each day. Continue to use your classroom bucket chart and your classroom bucket to reinforce the concepts of bucketfilling.

Finally, edit the Bucket Squad News to reflect your classroom activities for the week. Send home with the students or post on your website.

# BUCKET SQUAD NEWS

## SESSION EIGHT

**Dear Parent or Guardian:**

This week the bucket squad learned all about being a spy! We started out by playing a game of "I spy." Students had to be observant and spy a change in their classmates or teacher.

Next we talked about what it means to be a bucket detective. What clues do people give about whether or not they have a full or empty bucket? If we notice the clues and spy someone that may have an empty bucket, what actions can we take to help fill the other's bucket?

Learning to be observant of other people's feelings helps children to develop the important skills of reading body language and showing empathy for peers. This will help the Bucket Squad to be better friends to others and in turn, kids will see the Squad members as great friends to have!

Finally, being bucket detectives helps our entire school to be a positive place where kids feel good and ultimately, are more ready to learn. Imagine if everyone took time to be a bucket detective each day!

The Bucket Squad's goal for this week is to be a detective and notice when other people's buckets need filling. When they fill buckets by asking kids to play when they are left out or cheering someone up who is feeling down, they can cross off a square on their bucket chart. They have learned many ways to fill buckets; this week they get to choose the right way to fill a bucket based on the needs of the other person. This is an important life skill!

Sincerely,


Your Name, Title_____

Phone: _____

Email: _____

 **At Home Discussion:** Ask your child to describe what it means to be a bucket detective. Encourage her/him to be a bucket detective at home as well. How might it impact your family?

## YOUR BUCKET: A NO DIPPING ZONE!
### Skill Learned
How to replace negative self-talk with positive self-talk so our buckets stay full.

## OBJECTIVES:

⁊ Participants will:

⁊ Review being a bucket detective

⁊ Learn how self-talk can affect your own bucket

⁊ Practice kindness to self and self-acceptance

## SUPPLIES NEEDED:

⁊ Group rules from Session One

⁊ Group buckets from Session One

⁊ Check-in buckets and check-in sticks from Session Two

⁊ Book: *I'm Gonna Like Me* by Jamie Lee Curtis (for K-2nd) or other book that promotes self-esteem

⁊ Markers

⁊ Bucket Chart

## PREPARATION:

Before the group meeting, gather supplies and read through the curriculum. It is helpful to make several preparations prior to the group meeting. Here are a few suggestions:

**1.** Have the check-in buckets and check-in sticks out upon the students' arrival each week

**2.** Draw the bucket and dipper ahead of time

**3.** Copy the bucket chart for each group member

## GROUP CHECK IN: (5 to 10 minutes)

### How Full Is My Bucket?

**PART 1:** Using the check-in buckets and craft sticks from week two, have group members check-in. Sing the "How Are You?" song with younger kids.

**PART 2:** Give each student the individual bucket they made from Week One. Ask students to show you their Bucket Charts. Discuss how being a bucket detective worked during the last week.

⊘ What clues did you notice last week about buckets?

⊘ Without naming names, did you notice if some of the same kids seemed to have an empty bucket each day or for some, did it change a lot?

⊘ What did you do to fill buckets?

   ⊘ Did it work? How do you know?

   ⊘ Was there anybody who didn't let you fill their bucket?

   ⊘ How did you feel when you were able to use your detective skills to cheer someone up?

⊘ How could being a bucket detective help us make and keep friends?

**PART 3:** Fill their buckets! To reinforce the concept that we feel good about ourselves when we help other people who need their buckets filled, distribute bucketfilling items to each group member. Have the students place an item in their bucket for every square they checked off on their bucket chart. The Squad members will be adding to the items that are already in their buckets from previous weeks. Whether a group member adds two items to their bucket or twenty, it is up to the leader to set a positive tone and celebrate each accomplishment. This will help ensure that the group members realize they are working together as a team.

**Important:** It is okay if every square is crossed off. It shows in concrete actions that the more we fill other buckets, the fuller our own buckets become. The Bucket Chart is an honor system. It is important to model trust to the kids. However, it is also okay to encourage honesty by explaining that being dishonest may result in feelings of guilt or remorse. We wouldn't want them to dip into their own buckets in this way!

## OPENING ACTIVITY: (10 minutes)
### Play a quick game of "Step Forward If…"
Directions for play:

⊘ Stand in a circle

⊘ Have kids step forward without talking if the following statements are true for them. Then instruct the kids to step back into the circle.

⊘ Read the statement starting with the prompt, "Step forward if…"

⊘ Some questions may be more appropriate for older kids and some for younger. Choose those that work best for your group.

⊘ Older kids may enjoy the option of making up their own sentence prompts.

Leader says, "Step forward if…"

**1.** You are happy to be back at the Bucket Squad today!

**2.** Your favorite food is pizza.

**3.** You like to eat broccoli.

**4.** You like to play football at recess.

**5.** You like to play foursquare at recess.

**6.** You don't enjoy recess.

**7.** You like to read books.

**8.** You have a dog.

**9.** You don't have a pet.

**10.** You have chores at home (make bed, clear table, etc…).

**11.** You are good at sharing with friends.

**12.** You find it hard to share with siblings.

**13.** You like summer sports (swimming, biking, rollerblading, etc.).

**14.** You like winter sports (ice skating, sledding, skiing, etc.).

**15.** You believe you are good at something.

**16.** You can forgive yourself.

**17.** You like who you are.

**18.** You get frustrated with yourself.

**19.** You sometimes put yourself down (give examples if needed).

  Let the Squad Members know we all get frustrated with ourselves at times. However, when we put ourselves down with the things we say either out loud or silently in our thoughts, we are being bucket dippers. In other words, we take out the good feelings we have and empty our own buckets.

## LEARNING ACTIVITIES: (15 minutes)

**Say to the group**: "We have been filling buckets every week and watching our own buckets get full. They are holding a lot of good thoughts and feelings about us. During our second group meeting, we started filling our buckets with paper slips that said things we are good at and listed personal qualities that make us special. What were some of the things you liked about yourself? Is there anything you would add now? When we focus on those abilities, it helps us keep our good thoughts and feelings about ourselves safe inside our buckets. However, sometimes kids dip into their own buckets and empty out their good thoughts and feelings. Today, we are going to talk about how we can keep our buckets full.

### K-2nd Grades:

⟩ Read the story, *I'm Gonna Like Me,* by Jaimie Lee Curtis (Or choose another book with a similar theme.)

⟩ Use a check-in bucket while reading the story to illustrate how you can keep your good thoughts and feelings safe inside the bucket.

    – Fill the check-in bucket.

    – Each time the main character in the story says the words, "I'm gonna like me," talk about how she was kind to herself.

– What are some things kids might have said to themselves in that same situation?

– What would have happened to her bucket then? Illustrate dipping.

– How do you think her bucket looked at the beginning of the story?

– How do you think her bucket looked at the end of the story?

**3rd – 5th Grades:**

## PART 1:

⟩ On a large piece of poster paper or whiteboard, draw a dipper.

⟩ Brainstorm with the students to come up with some things that kids sometimes say or do to themselves that are bucket dipping. ("I'm stupid, I can't do that, I'm always messing up, no one likes me, etc.")

⟩ Write the words or phrases directly on the dipper OR give the students Post-its and have them write the words and phrases themselves and place them on the dipper.

⟩ Using a check-in bucket, show the kids how repeatedly putting ourselves down empties our bucket.

## PART 2:

⟩ Draw a large lid on poster paper or a whiteboard.

⟩ Ask the students to think of other words they may say to themselves when they make mistakes or feel badly that will protect their buckets and keep them full.

⟩ Write the words/phrases on the lid.

⟩ Or use Post-its to have kids write down the phrases and place them on the lid.

⟩ Have the kids practice replacing negative thoughts with positive ones.

⟩ Ask the students if they can identify any TV, movie, or book characters that are particularly good at thinking positively about themselves?

⟩ Is there a difference between bragging and just being positive?

Explain to the students that when we stop ourselves from saying or thinking negative beliefs and instead replace those thoughts with positive ones, it is like putting a lid on our bucket. We are helping to keep our good feelings about ourselves safe. We are protecting them.

## BUCKET CHART: (5 minutes)

**Weekly Goal: Keep our bucket full with positive self-talk.**

Each week, the Bucket Squad will be receiving a bucket chart to take home with them. Your goal for this week is to stop yourself (by using your lid) whenever you start to say something that isn't kind to yourself. Then, replace those negative thoughts with positive ones. Say, "I'm gonna like me even when...," or "I will try again, everyone makes mistakes." Whenever they do this, they can cross off a square on their Bucket Chart. When a parent or teacher catches them being positive with themselves, they can also cross off a square on their Bucket Chart. They should bring the chart with them to the next Bucket Squad meeting.

# CLOSING ACTIVITY: (3 minutes)

**K-1st Grade Option:** *The Bucket Squad Cheer!*

**2nd-5th Grade Option:** *The Bucket Squad Handshake!*

{ **Ask kids to pair up with a different partner this week to do the handshake!**
**Send home the Bucket Squad News.** }

 ## CLASSROOM TIPS:

If you are using this curriculum to teach and reinforce bucketfilling in the classroom, here are a few tips to adjust this lesson:

The format for this week adapts easily to the classroom. The idea of using a lid is conveyed through discussion and examples and does not need to be altered for the classroom setting. As a class, it would be great to have the students practice saying something positive about themselves each day. Kids often feel like they are bragging, but there is a difference between bragging and positive thinking. If the students can visualize it as protecting their buckets, they may feel more comfortable and in turn, will learn an important life skill.

You can also use this week's lesson to talk about making mistakes on tests or with school work. So many students dip into their own bucket when this happens. When mistakes happen in the classroom, you can ask kids to come up with reassuring words to give as examples to the class. Every time the class offers reassuring words when a student makes a mistake, such as, "Everyone makes mistakes, or mistakes will help me learn more," you can add to your classroom bucket! Perhaps this could be a class chant for the week so that individual students do not feel singled out, but rather the whole group says it whenever there is a mistake in class.

How full is your classroom bucket? What has the impact of the past nine weeks been on your class? This can be a great time to check in with the kids regarding their individual buckets. If you had your students complete an individual bucket chart during week two to show you how full their bucket was, repeat the activity this week. Compare your students' individual buckets from week two. How have they changed? As they have become better at bucketfilling, have they noticed their own buckets getting fuller? Collect their buckets and compare them from week two. If you identify individual students you are concerned about, follow up and find out what is causing their buckets to be low or empty. Acknowledge the students who have seen growth in their buckets as well.

Finally, edit the Bucket Squad News to reflect your classroom activities. Send it home with your students or post to your classroom website.

# BUCKET SQUAD NEWS
## SESSION NINE

**Dear Parent or Guardian:**

The bucket squad has been working hard during the last several weeks to fill other people's buckets and in turn, their own buckets have been filling as well. However, sometimes people take their own good feelings out of their buckets by putting themselves down. Today, we learned that we can help keep our buckets full by paying attention to what we tell ourselves out loud or privately in our thoughts.

The younger kids read a story about the importance of liking themselves just the way they are!

The older kids spent time discussing examples of what kids sometimes say to themselves that dip into their own bucket and then talked about phrases they could say instead that would keep their buckets full. We also talked about TV, movie, or book characters they know and whether or not these characters are good at keeping their buckets full by being positive or if they dip into their own bucket.

The students' goal for this week is to work hard to say positive affirmations to themselves when they make a mistake or are feeling down. This isn't something that you will easily monitor for them, but it is important for them to be self aware and willing to monitor it themselves. If they do say negative phrases out loud, encourage your child to come up with an alternative way of thinking about the situation and phrase it more positively.

Sincerely,

Your Name, Title_____

Phone: _____

Email: _____

{ **At home discussion:** Whenever possible, model the importance of being accepting of who you are. Show that mistakes are opportunities to learn! }

## THE BUCKET SQUAD CELEBRATES!
### Skill Learned
It is important to celebrate our accomplishments.

## OBJECTIVE:
⍟ Participants will:

⍟ Review self-talk and how it affects your own bucket.

⍟ Review all the bucketfilling skills we learned!

⍟ Celebrate our success at filling buckets and making a positive difference in our school.

## SUPPLIES NEEDED:
⍟ Group rules from Session One

⍟ Group buckets from Session One

⍟ Check-in buckets and check-in sticks from Session Two

⍟ Lids for their buckets

⍟ Beach ball or plastic ball

⍟ Written notes for each Bucket Squad Member

## PREPARATION:
Before the group meeting, gather supplies and read through the curriculum. It is helpful to make several preparations prior to the group meeting. Here are a few suggestions:

**1.** Have the check-in buckets and check-in sticks out upon the students' arrival each week.

**2.** Make lids for the individual buckets out of card stock or another material of your choice.

**3.** Write the review questions on the ball.

**4.** Write your personal notes to each team member.

## GROUP CHECK IN: (5 to 10 minutes)

### How Full Is My Bucket?

**PART 1:** Using the check-in buckets and craft sticks from week two, have group members check in. Sing the "How Are You?" song with younger kids.

**PART 2:** Give each student the individual bucket they made from Session One. Ask students to show you their Bucket Charts. Discuss whether or not they were able to keep a lid on their bucket by thinking and saying positive thoughts to themselves.

⍟ Did you catch yourself when you were going to say or think something negative? Were you able to stop yourself?

⍟ Can you name one negative thought you turned around to become positive?

✎ How did it feel?

✎ If you did this every day, how do you think it would affect your bucket?

✎ When you feel happier, do you think you treat other people with more kindness? Why?

**PART 3:** Instead of filling their buckets this week, have the students make a lid for their individual buckets. You can use pieces of cardstock or a plastic lid from another container. Be creative and make sure it is sturdy. For younger students, you might find it helpful to have the lids pre-made or cut out ahead of time. For older students, you can decide whether to have them make the lid during group time or not. Have students write positive statements about themselves on the lid and then put it over their buckets. I like to add a slit in the lid so they can see that they are able to still accept bucketfilling actions from others. But at the same time, the lid creates a barrier for bucket dipping. The better we feel about ourselves, the more likely we are to not allow someone else to take away our good feelings. This is a tangible reinforcement of these concepts!

## OPENING ACTIVITY: (10 minutes)

### Have a Ball!

Since today is the last official group meeting, it is a great day to review all of the bucketfilling skills the kids have learned! Before group, write down questions and prompts on a ball (large plastic balls or beach balls work well). Have younger students sit in a circle and take turns rolling the ball. Older students can stand in a circle and take turns tossing the ball. When a student catches the ball, they should look to see where their left thumb is located. Whatever question is closest to their thumb is the question they read aloud and answer. Once they are finished, they roll or toss the ball to another player.

| What does an invisible bucket hold? | Who has a bucket? | What does it mean if a bucket is empty or low? |
|---|---|---|
| What does it mean if someone has a full bucket? | Name 2 clues that someone might reveal if their bucket is low or empty. | Name 2 clues that someone might reveal if their bucket is full. |
| Do the bucket squad cheer or handshake. | What is bucketdipping? | Name the 3 parts of an "it dips" message. |
| Give and example of an "it dips" message. | Give the person on your right a friendly greeting. | Show us what good listening looks like. How does listening fill buckets? |
| Give the person on your left a genuine compliment. | How does being a bucket filler help your entire school? | Name one of your qualities or talents that you like. |
| Why do you need to put a lid on your bucket? | How is sharing and taking turns examples of cooperation? | Name two ways you can fill someone's bucket. |

# LEARNING ACTIVITIES: (15 minutes)

## Count the Buckets!

Have each child count the contents in her/his weekly bucket. How many times have they used bucketfilling during the past 10 weeks? Record each child's total number and add them together for a group total. Look at all the times the Squad helped others feel good! You can use the table below to record the answers:

Utilize this discussion time and the bucket contents as a visual prop to drive home what an amazing difference the kids have made! This is a great way to empower the kids to continue their bucketfilling behaviors and build their self-esteem in the process.

## ISN'T IT AMAZING WHAT A COMMITTED GROUP OF BUCKET FILLERS CAN DO!

| Name | How many times were you a bucket filler? |
|---|---|
|  |  |
|  |  |
|  |  |
|  |  |
|  |  |
|  |  |
| Group Total |  |

## FILL THEIR BUCKETS! (5 to 10 minutes)

Give each child their bucket to take home with them this week. You can either collect the filling items to use with future groups or send it home with the current class members.

This week, instead of a bucket chart, it is the leader's turn to formally fill each Squad member's bucket. Ahead of time, write a personal note describing for each child how you have seen them grow as a bucket filler. Encourage them to continue to be bucket fillers and emphasize how proud you are of them. Place each note in their bucket. You can either read these notes out loud or ask the kids to read them privately later (depending on their age). Or if you do not have time to write notes, you can verbally praise each child instead. However you choose to do this is up to you! You can also add a little treat or a coupon for a special event spent with you, like having lunch together.

Finally, give each student an official Bucket Squad Certificate! (Appendix B)

## CLOSING ACTIVITY: (10 minutes)

To end the day, play a final game of Compliment Toss (introduced in session five). This time, they will play the game twice.

⁊ The first time, they will say, "One thing I am proud of myself for is…"

⁊ The second time, they will say, "One thing I liked about being in the Bucket Squad is…"

⁊ The last time they will say, "I will continue to be a bucket filler because…!"

**K-1st Grade Option:** *The Bucket Squad Cheer!*

**2nd-5th Grade Option:** *The Bucket Squad Handshake!*

Do the final cheer or handshake! Send the kids home with:

**1.** Their individual buckets

**2.** Your note

**3.** Their certificate

**4.** The final Bucket Squad News

 ## CLASSROOM TIPS:

If you are using this curriculum to teach and reinforce bucketfilling in the classroom, here are a few tips to adjust this lesson:

What an amazing journey your class has been on for the past 10 weeks! The purpose of this session is to celebrate all that the kids have learned and the bucketfilling they have accomplished. But, it is also about encouraging them to continue to be bucket fillers beyond the end of the curriculum.

Play "Have a Ball" with your class. You can either use one ball for the entire classroom or you can use a couple of balls and divide the class into two or more groups. This is a great game for review. You can keep this ball and pull it out at different times during the school year to continue to reinforce the importance of being bucket fillers.

Count the contents of your classroom bucket! How many times have the kids in your class filled each other's buckets during the past several weeks? It could be fun to hold a "guess the number" contest prior to counting! Celebrate the number and reinforce how each of them had an important part in the teamwork that made this achievement possible.

*Let's celebrate our success at filling buckets and making a positive difference in our school!*

Fill their buckets! Designate a special chair in the classroom for the bucket filler of the day. Choose someone in your classroom to celebrate. Have the kids say one way that this student filled their buckets. Make sure that every child gets a turn before the school year is over.

Finally, continue to draw upon the bucketfilling language and examples of these important social skills when they occur in your classroom or when reading stories to the class. Tell your students that you will be looking for them to continue to be bucket fillers and that you will occasionally plan a special bucketfilling activity for your class. You can continue to fill a classroom bucket if you choose.

Send the last Bucket Squad News home to parents or post on your website. Thanks for creating a bucketfilling classroom! The effects of your efforts will stretch far beyond this school year and positively impact your students for years to come.

# BUCKET SQUAD NEWS
## SESSION TEN

### Dear Parent or Guardian:

Today was our last Bucket Squad group meeting. We did several fun activities to end our weeks of hard work!

We started the group by reviewing how important it is to think and say positive affirmations about ourselves. The students wrote positive messages on a lid that they can now keep on their individual buckets. The lid is a reminder for the students to protect their good thoughts and feelings.

After making our lids, we played a review game with a ball. We passed a ball around with questions written on it. When we caught the ball, we had to answer the question that was closest to our left thumb. This gave us a chance to remember all of the important ways we have learned to be bucket fillers.

We received a special note today from our group leader. Our notes describe how good at bucketfilling we have become! These notes are now part of our buckets. We also got to take our buckets home with us today and received a bucket squad certificate.

Sincerely,

Your Name, Title_____

Phone: _____

Email: _____

Thank you so much for sharing your children with me during the last ten weeks. I have enjoyed getting to know each of them and I am so pleased with all that they have learned. Together, they filled _____ buckets (the number we totaled in group today). They have made a positive impact in our school and in turn, I hope that their self-confidence and constructive self-directed feelings have also grown.

**At Home Discussion:** Talk to your child about how s/he can continue to fill buckets both at home and at school. Also continue to reinforce the bucketfilling skills whenever you see them! Thanks for all your support!

**Appendix A: The Bucket Chart**

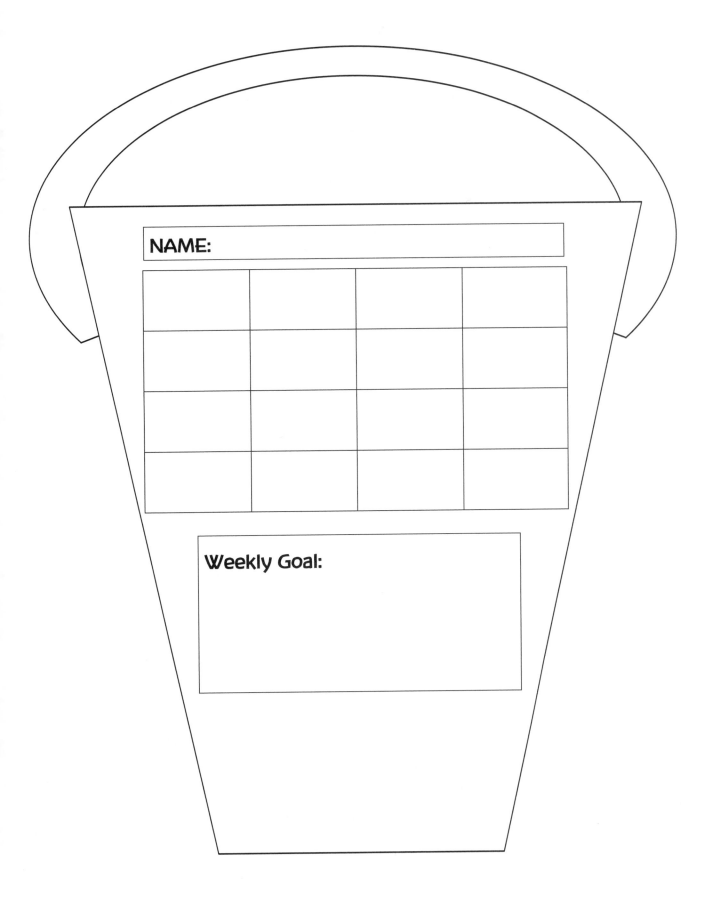

NAME:

Weekly Goal:

# CONGRATULATIONS!

_____

(PARTICIPANT'S NAME)

Has become an official lifetime team member of the

_____

(SCHOOL'S NAME)

# BUCKET SQUAD

Thanks for learning how to be an amazing bucket filler!
With your continued dedication as an official Bucket
Squad team member, our school and world
will become even more kind...

**One Bucket at a Time!**

# ABOUT THE AUTHOR

**Lisa Hansen** is a licensed school counselor in Minnesota. She has seven years experience working as an elementary school counselor and is currently in her third year as a high school counselor. Lisa has also worked extensively with grieving children and teens for over 10 years as a co-director for a children's grief support program in the Twin Cities. Lisa has a degree in Psychology and Master's degree in Counseling from the University of Wisconsin – Stout.

Lisa lives in Farmington, Minnesota with her husband, Troy. Together, they are raising three bucket-filling children, Paige, Chaise, and Dane.

## ❮ Acknowledgements ❯

Thank you to the students of Lakeview Elementary School in Lakeville, MN who participated in my first Bucket Squad groups and to the staff and parents who embraced the bucketfilling concepts.

Thanks to Jennifer Simmonds who encouraged me to write a curriculum and is one of the most amazing bucket fillers I know!

Thank you to my husband, Troy who has been an unwavering partner to me and overflows my bucket with his kindness and love. You have taken wonderful care of our kids while I worked on this project.

And a special thank you to Carol McCloud who wrote the books that inspired the concept of the Bucket Squad and for her support of this project.